JESUS BRAND™
SPIRITUALITY

HE WANTS HIS RELIGION BACK

KEN WILSON

THOMAS NELSON
Since 1798

NASHVILLE   DALLAS   MEXICO CITY   RIO DE JANEIRO   BEIJING

Jesus Brand Spirituality
© 2008 by Ken Wilson

Published in Nashville, Tennessee, by Thomas Nelson. Thomas Nelson is a registered trademark of Thomas Nelson, Inc.

Thomas Nelson, Inc., titles may be purchased in bulk for educational, business, fund-raising, or sales promotional use. For information, please e-mail SpecialMarkets@ThomasNelson.com.

All Scripture quotations, unless otherwise indicated, are taken from the HOLY BIBLE, TODAY'S NEW INTERNATIONAL VERSION®. 2001, 2005 by International Bible Society. Used by permission of Zondervan. All rights reserved.

Scripture quotations marked (NIV) are taken from the HOLY BIBLE, NEW INTERNATIONAL VERSION®. NIV®. © 1973, 1978, 1984 by International Bible Society. Used by permission of Zondervan. All rights reserved.

Scripture quotations marked NKJV are taken from the THE NEW KING JAMES VERSION. © 1982 by Thomas Nelson, Inc. Used by permission. All rights reserved.

Some details in the personal stories told in this book have been changed to protect the privacy of the individuals involved.

Library of Congress Cataloging-in-Publication Data

Available upon request.
ISBN: 978-08-8499-2053-0 (U.S. Edition)
ISBN: 978-08499-2111-7 (International Edition)

Printed in the United States of America

08 09 10 11 12 QW 9 8 7 6 5 4 3 2 1

FOR BRIAN MARTIN AND DICK BIEBER,
WHO GOT ME STARTED,
AND NANCY, WHO LED THE WAY

CONTENTS

FOREWORD

by Phyllis Tickle

I am not much given to tears, not ordinarily anyway. For joy? Yes. I can, and sometimes do, cry for joy. Grief and sorrow? We all can cry over them. We all do. And beauty. Always for beauty. But the truth of the thing is that I don't have a definition for beauty. Neither, of course, do philosophers or aestheticians, when one gets right down to it. In fact, with beauty, almost all of us have to fall back into the tired old saw of "I don't know how to describe it, but I know it when I see it."

With beauty, that trite saying means for me that I recognize immediately the strange stillness that always surrounds beauty, like an opening in space and time, making a corona or aura around it. I know by perceived sensation the way beauty goes straight to my thorax when it enters me, rising only later, if at all, to my head. I know the union I feel, if just for a few moments, with all things when I am in the presence of beauty. And I know that beauty makes me tear up just for the wonder of its being possible—just for the sheer miracle that the stuff of creation can be so arranged as to become this that I receive as beauty.

This is not a beautiful book (though it is hardly an ugly one). This, instead, is a book that contains niches and corridors and apses of beauty that catch my thorax and make me feel the salt and burn of beauty rising. The faith we Christians claim has been so dented and chipped and discolored by the centuries, so institutionalized and codified and doctrinalized, so written upon and then so over-written into palimpsest, that there are few Christians who still can discern the contours of the original. There are fewer still who know, and can persuasively teach, that Christianity was only and always just the container, the wrapping paper being used in shipment through the centuries of time. It is the Jesus beyond dent or chip or discoloring that is the beauty. It is the Jesus beyond the doctrine and the clashing commentary that is beauty.

I have known Ken Wilson for several years, have held in deep gratitude our friendship and his constancy, have sought his counsel, and have profited from his candor and forthrightness. I have also yearned—a strong word, *yearned,* but an apt one in this context. I have yearned for him to set down on paper the words that follow here. But even having heard Ken Wilson preach, having spent innumerable hours with him in both conversation and correspondence, I was still unprepared for the result of this transposing of his scholarship and insights from oral delivery to printed presentation. The oral can be heard (and now reheard, thanks to technology), but in a print culture, it can never be considered with the same deliberateness or vulnerability as can the read words. The heard is external in formation; the read is first taken in and then sounded; and that principle makes a substantial difference always.

Wilson writes with an easy pen and a light, almost jovial, touch. Sometimes one suspects a bit of tongue is in his cheek. Sometimes one knows he is being deliberately droll. And sometimes he is just a very, very good storyteller. Always he is Jesus'. And because he is secure in that positioning, he sees as naturally and unselfconsciously as a child contemplating his mother or her father. Why this matters—why its recording here is shot through with beauty—is that Jesus loves Ken.

This book, in effect, is a love story between one man and one Jesus. The distinction to be made between this story and all the others I have ever read is that this one is not entirely a monologue. In this one, we catch snatches of a two-way conversation. In this one, there are glimpses of a present Jesus as well as of a Jesus memorialized in photographs or word portraits; and that distinction makes a telling difference here.

But I want to say one more thing before I close this introduction to pages that, truth be told, need no preamble. I want to say that quite apart from the delight of these pages, there is a vital theme running through them, one that is itself beautiful the way a clear stream in a mountain valley is full and beautiful. The streambed is that the experience and exercise of spirituality are inherent in all human beings. The stream is that Christian spirituality is just that— Christian. Or, as Ken Wilson would have it, it is Jesus Brand; and that truth makes the entire difference. Here. Everywhere. Always.

Phyllis Tickle

1
RECLAIMING THE PILGRIMS' PATH

Jesus wants his religion back. And he wants it back from the orthodox, the Bible-believing, and the defenders of faith as much as from anyone else. So it can be for the world again.

I've been in the God business for more than thirty years. Never have I seen or personally experienced such angst over what it means to be associated with Jesus of Nazareth. If my fascination with Jesus had started today rather than so many years ago, I wonder what I would do with it. How would I begin to pursue faith today? I'll tell you what would put me off. I'd be repelled by the witch's brew of politics, cultural conflict, moralism, and religious meanness that seems so closely connected with those who count themselves the special friends of Jesus. It's a crowd that makes me nervous. Beneath all the talk of moral values and high principles, I don't think I could get over the hissing sound.

I would be deterred by the impression that the more people organize their lives around Jesus, the more likely they are to become defensive, prickly, and dogmatic about their beliefs. I'd have to stuff my questions, curb my curiosity, and be willing to get with the program. I'd have to mindlessly accept some package deal agreed on by the gatekeepers of orthodoxy—virgin birth, heaven and hell, Jesus as the only way, the Bible as the unquestioned Word of God—where would it stop?

Rather than wander onto that landscape, I think I'd keep my interest in Jesus to myself. I might watch one of those public broadcasting specials that turn up every Easter, but I'd avoid anything that would pull me in too deep, for fear of the alligators in the swamp of contemporary religion. Jesus, I'm afraid, would remain unexplored territory.

Perhaps you have a fully formed "Christian identity." You've invested too much of your life in the pursuit of Jesus to back out now. But something's gnawing at you that you can't quite put into words. It's not that you're having a crisis of faith so much as it feels like faith itself is in crisis. The faith that has worked for you isn't working for your son, your daughter, or other loved ones. And you can't *imagine* it working for them. That is, you can't imagine them jumping through all the hoops to participate in the form of faith you find yourself in.

SOMETHING'S GNAWING AT YOU THAT YOU CAN'T QUITE PUT INTO WORDS. IT'S NOT THAT YOU'RE HAVING A CRISIS OF FAITH SO MUCH AS IT FEELS LIKE FAITH ITSELF IS IN CRISIS.

I have a friend who is an oceanographer. There's a rhapsodic quality to his engagement with the ocean. Because he's a scientist, it seems to him patently ridiculous to embrace a religion on good authority before he can prove its worthiness for himself. So does the thought of becoming a Christian when those most vocally claiming the label are least likely to care about the earth—the one that gives him the mystical shivers.

Yet my oceanographer friend is drawn to Jesus of Nazareth. He speaks openly of his admiration for Charles Darwin and Jesus— Darwin for helping us see the profound relationship among all living things; Jesus for teaching us to love our enemies and thus giving us a way to be united with each other. But where does my friend go from here with his inclination toward Jesus when so much associated with the name of Jesus is repugnant to him?

Jesus is a presence distinct from the religion that represents him.[1] We are drawn to him (or not) for reasons that defy easy explanation. But being drawn to Jesus doesn't necessarily mean buying the package of faith as defined by those with the biggest bullhorns. It may be the most subtle of inclinations. Something in us leans in his direction. Are we being pulled? That's for each of us to decide. What's important is the movement—the leaning toward as if to listen, to object, to surrender, to question, to help. That's the quivering nerve of what makes Jesus a movement maker: he *moves* people.

Maybe it's time to adjust some of the conventional assumptions about Christian faith. Maybe the starting point is as basic as people in motion, moving toward Jesus.

---

1. Strictly speaking, we can't easily separate our understanding of Jesus from the community that represents him; after all, it was his intention to form a community that would make him known. Without such a community, we wouldn't know anything about him. But it is important that we learn to distinguish between Jesus and the community that bears his name, so we can realize that it has the potential both to represent him well and to horribly misrepresent him.

AN ALTERNATIVE VIEW

Let's do a little thought experiment. What if we set aside all the politics, programs, pathways, and perspectives that have shaped the current forms of Christian faith? What if we stripped off the defining labels for now—orthodox, secular, progressive, conservative, liberal—duly noting them as touching on important issues, but not our present concern?

For the purpose of our experiment, let's think of Jesus as the magnetic presence buried beneath the movements that represent him. He is the attractor who is obscured as much as he is revealed by the labels that define us in relation to him. Let's imagine ourselves in relation to Jesus—all of us who feel drawn to Jesus in some way—as being neither on the outside of faith looking in, nor on the inside looking out, nor at one of the stages of a predetermined four-stage linear progression of belief.

Instead, let's imagine ourselves at various points in relation to an imagined center, like pilgrims coming from the north, south, east, and west and every point in between to a holy city. Only we aren't pilgrims in search of a city so much as pilgrims in search of an influence, Jesus of Nazareth. Some of us are here, others there. Some are running, walking, milling about, traveling in groups or singly, doubting or believing—but all of us are within range of his attractive pull. Because we come from different points of origin, we take many paths to our destination. The closer we get to the center, the more our paths converge. But for now, the only concern each of us shares is this: how can we take "one step closer to knowing,"[2] one step closer to that center we're longing for?

---

2. The phrase "one step closer to knowing" is the haunting title of a song from the album *How to Dismantle an Atomic Bomb* by U2.

THE PILGRIMS' PATH: EARTHY, MYSTICAL, CURIOUS

"Jesus brand spirituality" is the phrase I'm using to describe a path that such a pilgrim might take from wherever he or she happens to be now, toward that imagined center. It is stripped down, like the itinerant wonder-worker from Nazareth: *earthy* as he was, keeping company with the people of the land and concerned to make this world a better one; *mystical,* engaging this life with wide-eyed wonder and eager for intimacy with the divine; and *curious,* prone to question and to explore reality even if it meant offending religious sensibilities.

JESUS BRAND SPIRITUALITY IS A WAY OF LIVING THAT JESUS MODELED AS A FELLOW PILGRIM.

Jesus brand spirituality is a way of living that Jesus modeled as a fellow pilgrim. He forged a path we can follow.

I realize the word *brand* can be used in a negative sense, as short-hand for the crass attempt to "sell" Jesus in a consumer culture.[3] But there are two positive senses in which Jesus *is* a kind of brand. First, like a brand-name product, Jesus has a distinct as opposed to a generic identity. Jesus brand spirituality is not a generic spirituality concerned with processes that can support any number of outcomes. It's about forming certain kinds of persons, capable of certain kinds of deeds, creating a certain kind of world: persons, deeds, and a world infused by love, properly understood.

Second, the term *brand* also implies that his is a spirituality over

---

3. For example, see Tyler Wigg Stevenson's critique in *Brand Jesus* (New York: Seabury, 2007).

which Jesus exercises proprietary rights. It shouldn't be surprising that a brand as powerful as Jesus' would be subject to trademark infringement. This has happened repeatedly over the centuries. The Roman Empire saw in the Jesus movement a potentially unifying force for the empire and infringed on the brand. Political agendas from the left and the right throughout history have gained ascendancy by infringing on the Jesus brand.

I'm the product of the Jesus Movement, a spiritual awakening fueled by baby boomers in the anti-institutional, countercultural phenomenon of the 1960s and early 1970s. Many of us were anti-war, ecologically minded, and eager to forge a new spiritual path radically centered on the person of Jesus. By the 1980s and 1990s, those caught up in the Jesus Movement had cycled through periods of wild revivalism, experiments in communal living that attempted to create strong social bonds by an act of sheer collective will, and eventually an undiscerning alliance with conservative politics. I know from painful experience what it means to misrepresent the Jesus brand.

WE CAN ONLY HOPE JESUS WILL CONTINUE TO CHALLENGE EVERY EFFORT TO HIJACK HIS BRAND, BECAUSE HE IS, AND ALWAYS WILL BE, THE MAIN ATTRACTION.

In trademark law, the owner of a brand has a responsibility to challenge infringement efforts. We can only hope Jesus will continue to challenge every effort to hijack his brand, because he is, and always will be, the main attraction.

SPIRITUALITY: A SUBSET OF MESSY RELIGION

Spirituality is a word that gets used and abused with abandon. It's a subset of that messy business, religion. The Latin root of the word *religion* has to do with tying together, as in making connections; the *lig-* of *religion* appears in *ligament*, a form of connective tissue.

I use the word *religion* without apology, though it has fallen out of favor lately. I think our attempt to jettison the word is, not to put too fine a point on it, folly. We try to load all the things we don't like about religion onto the word itself, thinking that by dumping the word we can dump all its negative associations along with it. I think it would be wiser of us simply to accept the fact that life is messy, as is the human condition, as is anything touching on them.

As a context for understanding Jesus brand spirituality, let's locate it within the broader enterprise called religion.[4] Phyllis Tickle, author, lecturer, and founding religion editor for *Publishers Weekly*, describes religion as a rope that connects us to realities beyond, if very much around us.[5] The rope has three cords: spirituality, morality, and corporeality.

Corporeality[6] refers to the bodily, tangible, material things that constitute any religion, from the human institutions it generates to the physical rituals and symbols used to the deeds done in its name,

---

4. I think of it like this: humans are irreversibly religious. To be irreligious is an expression of our religious tendencies. Our task, before God, is not to jettison religion any more than it is to jettison human culture. God wants to redeem our humanity, which means we have to struggle toward a redeemed religion.

5. From a lecture titled "Today's Church in America, Part One," presented by Phyllis Tickle, Calvary Episcopal Church, Memphis, TN, January 19, 2007.

6. Corporeal, as in "of or relating to the body," and by extension, the physical and material, as distinguished from the spiritual apsects of religion; it also implies "corporate" in contrast with "individual."

for better or worse. It is the literal stuff of religion. This is the part of religion we'd just as soon didn't exist. It's the part we try to deny when we say, "I'm spiritual, but not religious." We might just as well say, "I'm mind but not body."

This strand is the messiest part of religion. It's what grabs the headlines, such as EPISCOPAL CHURCH DIVIDES OVER LATEST CONTRO-VERSY, and we all roll our eyes. It's only messy because it involves us as we are, connecting us as it does to the physical, material world. We can try to cut this limb off the tree of religion, but we should keep in mind that it's the limb we're sitting on when we wield the chain saw. Still, it's worth remembering that the mess associated with this part of religion is a mess of our own and not of God's making.

Morality refers to the answer any religion offers to the question, "How should we then live?"[7] This includes abortion, gay marriage, and gender issues—many of our hot-button moral concerns. *Morality* has become a wedge word since the self-righteous majority started using it to promote their particular version, a version that conveniently leaves out concern for the poor and justice for the oppressed. But the fact that we count this use of morality as "bad" reveals the fact that we can't avoid it. Religion is about truth and beauty and ultimate realities like good and evil. Even though we often get it wrong, morality is an inescapable concern of religion.

Which brings us to *spirituality*, something intertwined with morality and corporeality, but also, thankfully, something we can distinguish from these. Spirituality is about living a life informed

---

7. This question is borrowed from the title of Francis Schaeffer's insightful book, *How Should We Then Live: The Decline of Western Thought and Culture* (Wheaton, IL: Crossway, 1976).

and infused by spirit, however *spirit* is understood. To adapt a use of Stephen Hawking's phrase, spirituality is "the fire in the equations" of religion.[8] Of the three cords that constitute religion—corporeality, morality, and spirituality—spirituality has most to do with the connection itself between the human and the divine. If corporeality is the copper wire of an electrical circuit and morality a switch that directs it, then spirituality is the electrons inexplicably exciting each other as the current pulses through the wire.

The three cords of the religion rope are held together by a casing, like the clear plastic casing that holds the strands of a rope together and keeps the water out. The casing of any religion is the story it tells about the way the world works. *Once upon a time, God made himself a world, and he loved the world so much that . . .* Everything else about religion makes sense only in the context of the story it tells about the world. The story is the forest of religion; everything else is trees. There's room for us in any religion only if there's a place for us in the story it tells.

Any religion will be judged by the story it tells about the world and our place in it. Stories either hold together or fall apart. They either strike us as true or not. They either help us make sense of reality or they don't.

Jesus brand spirituality is but one cord among the connections Jesus came to make between us and God, between us and other human beings, between us and all living things. It informs issues of morality and corporeality, but it is distinct from both, so the issues

---

8. For an excellent discussion of what Stephen Hawking meant by this phrase, read Kitty Ferguson, *The Fire in the Equations: Science, Religion, and the Search for God* (Princeton, NJ: Templeton Foundation, 2004).

pertaining to these cords will be largely ignored here. Perhaps we could all use a rest from them anyway. If spirituality is the fire in the equations of religion, then we could all use the added warmth and light when the time comes to face these thorny questions.

After all the jostling and debating and advocating and thrashing about that comes with the concerns of religion, there comes a moment of truth when we sit by ourselves alone in a room and wonder whether God exists; we wonder what difference his existence might make and whether and how we might reach out to God or discover that God is reaching out to us. This is the purview of spirituality.

A FOUR-DIMENSIONAL ORIENTATION
FOR PILGRIMAGE

What is the best way to describe what Jesus brand spirituality looks like in practical terms so we can find our way on this path? If we all started from the same place, we could describe the path as an engineer might. We could consider the four steps of a clearly defined linear progression. That makes for a good membership class in church, but it rarely meets us where we find ourselves, which is all over the map. We don't all start from the same point of origin. We each have a different religious history; we each have different impressions of Jesus that draw or repel us at different times. The next step closer to knowing that awaits you is not likely to be the next step closer to knowing that awaits me.

I hope instead to provide an orientation that you can use to form a bigger picture of the spirituality Jesus offers and from which you can discern, as long as you find it useful, the answer to the pilgrims' question, "Which way do I go to take one step closer to knowing, one step closer to the center?"

This orientation is organized around four dimensions of spirituality. By "dimensions," I mean aspects of reality, as in the four dimensions of the space-time fabric: length, width, height, and time. But the four dimensions I've selected to describe Jesus brand spirituality are *active, contemplative, biblical,* and *communal.*

I'll describe these dimensions one at a time, but the sequence is not important. These four dimensions of spirituality are as interdependent as the four space-time dimensions. We separate them to examine them, but as soon as we're done, they reconnect. We must resist the temptation to force-fit these into a preordered path: "First, we take the active step, then the contemplative," and so on. It doesn't work like that. Depending on where we find ourselves on this pilgrimage, we may be drawn to one dimension or the other first or next. But as we move forward into one dimension of Jesus brand spirituality, our understanding of all the others will be affected because they are four dimensions of one reality.

Why these particular dimensions? Because they are integral. Each is an essential part of spirituality—distinguishable in representing a discrete aspect, yet interdependent in affecting and being affected by the others. They also emerge naturally from the spiritual path of Jesus himself.

After all the adoration that has understandably attended Jesus through the centuries, we sometimes forget that Jesus was a fully human being.[9] This means that Jesus arrived at a kind of spirituality—

---

9. I don't think you've gone deep enough into the mystery of Jesus until you consider the possibility that he was also fully divine; much recorded in the Gospels intimates this.

a way of life informed and infused by spirit—in the way human beings do. He was part of a faith community that modeled various approaches; he engaged a sacred text that was at the center of that community's faith and practice; he was curious, asking questions of his elders in the temple; he explored the realms of prayer; and he acted in accordance with his growing understanding. As one of the Gospels says it, "As Jesus grew up, he increased in wisdom and in favor with God and people" (Luke 2:52).[10] Jesus' emerging spirituality was active, contemplative, biblical, and communal.

Active

Jesus' spirituality was *active* because things were happening. Events were rapidly unfolding in Israel that called for a response. The life of Jesus shows us that the God connection doesn't just occur while we're sitting in a monastery. It happens while life is busy before us, demanding our immediate attention.

It's no accident that Jesus unveiled his teaching while on the move from village to village, person to person, problem to problem, as a kind of commentary on his actions—gathering the poor and the outcast, healing the sick, threatening the powers-that-be, mobilizing a movement with an agenda.

His training method? Jesus invited curious onlookers to help him do what he was already doing so that his actions would have even greater impact. As we'll see, his actions were about addressing the pressing problems of his day. Anyone who wanted to learn more about him had to keep up with him first. There were no faith

---

10. This is the summary statement given when Jesus was found by his parents after staying behind in the temple to converse with the elders at the age of twelve.

quizzes to pass before you could help out; all it took was the willingness to go somewhere with Jesus because you liked what he was doing.

Whatever you believe about Jesus, whatever you think about this or that aspect of personal morality, however you feel about this or that Christian institution, Jesus has an agenda that inspires an active response to the problems of the world. You can draw one step closer to knowing him by understanding what he's up to and lending him a hand. Healing may even come your way as you help him heal the world.

Contemplative

Jesus' spirituality was also *contemplative*, because everyone feels there's more to this world than meets the eye. The world is a mystical playground where, according to the quantum physicists, the most elemental particles—things called quarks and muons and gluons and bosons—pop into and out of existence all the time. No, I don't understand it either. But the world is, according to those who can do the math, *not* as it seems.

Jesus was a mystic who prayed with his eyes open. His connection with God as his "Abba"[11] helped him to see the world through the lens of wonder. Jesus got up early in the morning and went out to lonely places, and there he prayed (Mark 1:35). When he came back from those times of prayer, you get the impression he must have been making some kind of conscious contact with the divine, because life seemed to blossom wherever he went.

---

11. *Abba* is the Aramaic term Jesus used for God, a term of familiar address not unlike our endearing term *Papa*.

So the way Jesus lived identifies him as someone who can teach us to pray. He can help us open our eyes to the world around us. He can help us understand the dimension of reality that we become aware of when we look out over the vast ocean, stop thinking normal thoughts, and just take it in, and something as deep as the ocean seems to be awakened within us.

Biblical

Jesus' spirituality was *biblical*, because Jesus was a master storyteller whose stories are incomprehensible apart from the bigger story in which they are told, the Bible being the primary source of this bigger story. Too often these days, the Bible is used as a kind of weapon to browbeat us into seeing things the way someone else wants us to see them. But in the hands of Jesus, the Bible became a different kind of book. It became a living thing full of the unexpected and the unconventional. It was a book Jesus turned against the browbeaters of his day with one hand, and with the other he comforted and consoled and energized those who had been bludgeoned with it.

The Bible in the hands of Jesus tells a story that has a place for us within it. If we could find our way into the Bible through the door Jesus entered, we might find the storyline of our lives and the world we live in changing for the better as a result.

Communal

Jesus' spirituality was also *communal*, because spirituality is about forging connections between persons and between all living things, including, of course, God. If hell is the self-imposed absence of connections that God feared for us when he said, "It's not good for the human to be alone, I shall make him a sustainer beside him" (Gen. 2:18),[12] then heaven is what happens when all our connections here on earth light up with love.

On the pilgrims' path, there's a way of engaging the relational network that begins within God and includes all who are willing to participate; it remains open to those who are not participating for reasons of their own. It's important that we learn this part and soon; if we can't get along spread out as we are in many different locations around the center, how will we ever get along once we take a step closer and our paths start converging?

Pilgrims are shaped by their starting points as much as they are defined by their destination. Let's take the next step together by casting a wide-angle view across the vast landscape to help us understand the various places we're coming from.

---

12. Paraphrased by Robert Alter, in his excellent translation of Genesis. Alter notes that the Hebrew word *Adam* is a play on words with the Hebrew word for earth or dirt, in much the same way that the English word *human* is related to *humus* (the English word for dirt). Alter also argues that the traditional translation "helpmate" is too weak in its English connotations and that "sustainer" is better because the Hebrew word connotes active intervention on behalf of someone. See *Genesis: Translation and Commentary*, Robert Alter (New York: Norton, 1997), nn. 7, 18.

2
YOU ARE HERE

After Madalyn Murray O'Hair disappeared, outspoken atheism seemed to go into hibernation. This was a loss for all of us, because atheists are people who take God seriously enough to push off from him, which amounts to a form of contact. We have much to learn from atheists if we have ears to hear.

Sam Harris, Richard Dawkins, and Christopher Hitchens represent the return of outspoken atheism to the public square.[1] They make the case that religion is the greatest source of evil in the world and that we'd all be better off if we imagined and then brought into being a world without it. Their voice is amplified by the vengeful resurgence of religious intolerance expressed in religious warfare. No doubt about it, religious zeal *is* one of the great threats to human welfare these days.

---

1. See Sam Harris, *Letter to a Christian Nation* (New York: Knopf, 2006); Richard Dawkins, *The God Delusion* (New York: Houghton Mifflin, 2006); Christopher Hitchens, *God Is Not Great: How Religion Poisons Everything* (New York: Twelve Books, 2007).

The more you get to know any religion with a long history, including Christianity, the more you become aware of the extremes it produces: extreme good and extreme evil. One of the most understandable reasons for avoiding religion altogether is the feeling that we'd all be better off in the balanced middle zone occupied by less aggressive attempts at getting things *right* at any cost, including the well-being of people.

Harris, Dawkins, and Hitchens highlight the dissonance any thoughtful person feels in the contemporary religious climate about the pursuit of God on the Jesus path. Yet Jesus remains one of the most studied figures in history. His words continue to haunt us, whether we count ourselves among those who believe, those who doubt, or those who muddle their way forward, informed by both ways of seeing. "You have heard that it was said, 'Love your neighbor and hate your enemy.' But I tell you, 'Love your enemies and pray for those who persecute you'" (Matt. 5:43–44). Where did such words come from?

On a pilgrimage, only one step matters—the next one. But taking the next step requires sorting through a tangled web of impressions. To proceed, we do well to consider where it is we're coming from and what we might be bringing with us.

YOU ARE HERE

Whether or not we have a settled religious identity, we all have a collective religious history, even if a distant one. For all the complaining or rejoicing we may do about how secular our society has become, the fact remains that we are a very religious society. Belief in a personal God remains high. A recent survey reported that 47 percent of American non-Christians believe in the virgin birth.[2] Many of us have a parent or grandparent or close friend whom we consider to be devout. Our view of God is shaped by our religious history, so it's worth locating ourselves on the map, so to speak. A pilgrimage always begins where we are.

The following graphic attempts to simplify the incredibly diverse field of religion to something we can consider in a kind of shorthand. It is a handy tool, which means it reduces a complex reality into manageable categories. The reduction process squeezes out important aspects of reality. But if it's not handy, it's not helpful.

BIG PICTURE LANDSCAPE

JUDAISM	CHRISTIANITY
ISLAM	EASTERN RELIGIONS

Obviously, this graphic has a Western slant; Judaism has a much smaller number of adherents than are represented by these quadrants. Yet the religion of Israel has been so influential in Western

---

2. Nicholas D. Kristof, "Believe It, or Not," *New York Times*, August 15, 2003, http://query.nytimes.com/gst/fullpage.html?res=9800E7DE1730F936A2575BC0A9659C8B63 accessed November 5, 2007.

history as to justify its own quadrant. The Eastern religions quadrant represents a kind of "other" category that includes practices as diverse as Buddhism, Hinduism, Confucianism, Shintoism, animism, and practices grouped together under New Age.

CHRISTIANITY ON PILGRIMAGE

This being a book about Jesus brand spirituality, we are concerned with the Christianity quadrant,[3] which can be described with its own set of four. But first, we'll sprint through more than two millennia of Christian history to help us get our bearings along the axis of time. This exercise reveals that Christianity itself has been on a pilgrimage. Throughout history, the Jesus movement has morphed into new forms, even as older forms remain and adapt.

In the first generation, Jesus left behind a messianic movement among the Jewish people. Within decades, Christianity was on its way to becoming a global religion; it rapidly became the Gentile (non-Jewish) path to full inclusion with the God of Abraham. This new form of faith was facilitated by the road system of the Roman Empire because religion happens in the world, and changes in the world shape it powerfully.[4] Like all major shifts, this emerging faith was not without struggle—the anguish and

---

3. My friend Mark Kinzer, a leader within Messianic Judaism, places himself in the Judaism quadrant, though he claims Jesus of Nazareth as his promised Messiah. Many of his Jewish (as well as Christian) colleagues would much prefer that he place himself in the Christianity quadrant. It's a messy business, religion. See Mark S. Kinzer, Postmissionary Messianic Judaism (Grand Rapids: Brazos, 2005).

4. I'm indebted, once again, to the insights of Phyllis Tickle for much of this whirlwind tour through Christian history, especially the observations about the effect of technological advances on Christian thought.

controversy of its bloody struggle to survive are all over the pages of the New Testament.

In the fourth century, Christianity faced one of its biggest tests: success. The Roman Empire embraced Christian faith as the state-sanctioned religion. This in turn gave birth to the monastic movement as devout individuals sought a more spiritually enlivened form of faith removed from the trappings of the empire.

In the eleventh century, there was a split between Eastern and Western expressions of Christianity as Eastern Orthodoxy parted ways with the dominant Western form headquartered in Rome.

By the sixteenth century, the faith went through another massive shift—a reformation in reaction against Roman Catholicism that became known as Protestantism. This new form was facilitated by the printing press. It too was not without struggle, even bloodshed.

TWENTIETH-CENTURY FERMENT

Let's take a closer look at the twentieth century to understand more about the movements that shape the religious landscape today.

Christian fundamentalism was an early response to the juggernaut of modern science and rationalism that still influences the landscape today. Fundamentalism is an attempt to reassert a Christian worldview based on a literalist reading of the Bible, profiled against what were viewed as modern incursions toxic to faith. It was a movement that focused a great deal on orthodoxy, or correct belief, as defined by its leaders at the time. Other Christians responded to the rise of modernity by adapting to its more secular worldview; this was especially the case in the historic mainline denominations. Often, denominations were split by these divergent responses.

While this was under way, another movement broke out called Pentecostalism, marked by "speaking in tongues"[5] and a renewed emphasis on spiritual experience. It valued responsiveness to the impulse of the Spirit, whether that meant elevating the role of women or breaking down racial barriers—two marks of early Pentecostalism. In time, lacking a theology of its own and rejected by much of the established church, Pentecostals relied on the strict biblical system of fundamentalism,[6] even though this originally left little room for the Pentecostal emphasis on the Spirit and subjective experience. Pentecostalism remained a movement on the social fringe in the first half of the twentieth century, leaving the traditional churches of the Protestant Reformation and Catholicism untouched by its fervent appeal to experience. Much of Christian religion in the middle and upper classes lacked a vocabulary for spiritual experience.[7] Matters of the head ruled over matters of the heart, whether through a carefully reasoned fundamentalism or the increasing accommodation to the modern secular values found in more liberal, mainline churches.

Eventually, the Pentecostal movement began to spread beyond the lower socioeconomic class, bringing renewal movements to the mainline denominations, often referred to as Charismatic Renewal.[8]

5. Sociologists refer to this as *glossolalia*, a form of ecstatic speech with structure and a rudimentary syntax but whose meaning is usually unknown to the speaker.

6. For those keeping track, this system was called *dispensationalism* because it divided the biblical narrative into several distinct "dispensations," or eras.

7. Thanks to Phyllis Tickle for this insight.

8. The term *charismatic* derives from the Greek *charismata*, referring to the "spiritual gifts" referenced by Paul in 1 Corinthians 12–14 and other places.

In the mid-twentieth century, evangelicalism also began to separate from its more sectarian sibling, fundamentalism. Modern evangelicalism as an American phenomenon formed in the wake of popular evangelist Billy Graham.

As noted earlier, my adult faith connection occurred in the context of something called the Jesus Movement, a religious movement of the late 1960s counterculture, which was marked by anti-institutionalism and the somewhat delusional view by young members of the baby boomer generation that we were discovering Jesus for the first time apart from all the "dead churchianity" that had gone before. In time, this movement was absorbed into more established forms of evangelicalism and fundamentalism, adapting to the theology and view of Scripture in those settings.

The rise of the "religious right" in the 1980s is another significant development. This was a diverse movement shaped by political conservatism, including theologically conservative Roman Catholics, evangelicals, and fundamentalists, energized politically by the legalization of abortion on demand. This political movement has been strongest in rural and suburban communities. It should be remembered that many other Christians throughout the century leaned in the direction of liberalism.

Amid the great religious ferment of the twentieth century, Christian practice became much more diverse; institutional boundaries became less significant. A given denomination might have constituencies that leaned fundamentalist, while others leaned toward a loosening of historic faith, and still others explored a renewed interest in spiritual experience. These trends led to splits, mergers, and entirely new denominations. While Christianity as a whole held steady in the United States—some denominations losing members, others gaining—it underwent explosive growth in the developing world with significant gains in Africa, Latin America, and Southeast Asia.[9]

The robust and often dicey pilgrimage continues to this day. With significant developments like the Internet, where information exchange takes place at the speed of light, the resurgence of religious warfare, and a gathering global environmental crisis, it's likely we are in the midst of a new shift that will be recognized clearly only after it has taken place.

Which brings us to the landscape of Christianity today . . .

THE QUADRANTS OF CHRISTIANITY

LITURGICAL	SOCIAL JUSTICE
EVANGELICAL	RENEWALIST

9. While the God Is Dead movement was hitting mainline churches in the 1950s and observers began to speak of the "post-Christian" era, Pentecostalism was just beginning to make major gains overseas. Less dramatic movements such as the Jesus Movement and Charismatic Renewal began to reshape the landscape in the United States. Harvey Cox, professor of religion at Harvard, wrote a book on the spread of Pentecostalism, admitting that his and his colleagues' prediction of the end of the Christian faith couldn't have been more wrong (*Fire from Heaven: The Rise of Pentecostal Spirituality and the Reshaping of Religion in the Twenty-First Century* [New York: Addison-Wesley, 1994]).

The *liturgical* quadrant represents those church communions for whom the proper and faith-filled celebration of the liturgy (a prescribed order of service with heavy reliance on rituals, symbols, robes, candles, and set prayer) is of central importance. These communions include Roman Catholicism, Anglicanism, Eastern Orthodoxy, and some forms of Lutheranism, representing the longest-standing forms of Christian faith.

The *social justice* quadrant includes churches that preach what used to be called the "social gospel"[10] for its emphasis on social justice. Central to this identity is a concern to redress injustices like racism, sexism, and poverty; these are believed to be sustained by deeply imbedded social structures. Included are United Methodists, some Presbyterians, and "peace churches" such as Mennonites and Quakers. The African American churches that fueled the American civil rights movement were a powerful presence in the social justice quadrant.

The *evangelical*[11] quadrant represents those for whom the Bible, the "born again" conversion experience, and the preaching of the gospel are central identifiers. Less clearly defined than the groups within the liturgical and social justice quadrants, evangelicals include Baptists, Nazarenes, and Free Methodists, to name a few. Churches that lean toward a strictly literal interpretation of the Bible and a more sectarian approach are called *fundamentalist*. Both evangelical and fundamentalist churches are represented in this quadrant.

---

10. For more about the social gospel, see the seminal book of the movement: Walter Rauschenbusch, *Christianity and the Social Crisis* (New York: Macmillan, 1909).

11. Phyllis Tickle labeled this quadrant "conservative" in a lecture presented to First United Methodist Church of Ann Arbor, February 10, 2005.

The *renewalist*[12] quadrant is arguably a subset of evangelical, except that its sudden eruption and rapid expansion set it apart as a distinct expression.[13] It is marked by a renewed interest, one might even say craving, for experience. Pentecostalism is the major form, including the Church of God in Christ and the Assemblies of God. Charismatic Renewal, a movement crossing many traditional denominational boundaries, affected existing churches and formed new ones of its own.[14]

YOU ARE HERE: FAMILY BACKGROUND

Familiarity with this landscape helps orient us to the starting point of our own pilgrimage. Most of us base our impressions of Christianity—and by association, its founder—on a small sample of the landscape. The big picture provides a broader perspective for our own experience, offering options we might not have known about otherwise. If you grew up with the impression that Christianity is a religion of the privileged, it's helpful to know that Pentecostalism

12. *Renewalist* is a term used by the Pew Forum on Religion and Public Life to describe both Pentecostal and Charismatic Christianity; see their report "A 10-Country Survey of Pentecostals," October 2006, http://pewforum.org/surveys/pentecostal/ (accesssed December 14, 2007).

13. Renewalism is the fastest growing form of Christianity today, especially in the Southern hemisphere. Philip Jenkins, a religious scholar, has said that the typical Christian is no longer a white European or North American, as commonly thought, but a young single woman living in Nairobi, and, no doubt, Pentecostal in faith and practice. See Philip Jenkins, *The Next Christendom: The Coming of Global Christianity*, (London: Oxford University Press, rev. and exp. ed. 2007).

14. Charismatic renewal refers to newer versions of the Pentecostal movement that place less emphasis on the gift of tongues and make other cultural and theological adaptations, depending on a given context.

thrives among the underprivileged. If you are familiar with a faith tradition that cares little for social justice, it's enlightening to realize that this is not a characteristic of Christianity as a whole.

Most people have a family history that informs their perspective on Christianity. For example, my maternal grandmother grew up in the Church of England. My family tree has roots in the liturgical quadrant. My grandmother was raised in the Victorian era, when matters of religion were important, but not for polite conversation. In my house growing up, I can't recall reading bedtime Bible stories or praying at meals (though I'm sure this happened occasionally), and certainly not engaging in frank conversation about religious matters.

MOST OF US BASE OUR IMPRESSIONS OF CHRISTIANITY, AND BY ASSOCIATION ITS FOUNDER, ON A SMALL SAMPLE OF THE LANDSCAPE.

My father, whom I remember as a much less devout Episcopalian than my mother during my formative years, was the son of a man who was the "prodigal" in a very strict Plymouth Brethren family. This church tradition, rooted squarely in the fundamentalist section of the evangelical quadrant, came up with the theology behind the wildly popular Left Behind series of books about the end of the world.[15]

The relatives I've met on this side of the family are some of the kindest souls I know. My great-uncle Stuart prayed for me daily

---

15. The thirteen-book Left Behind series, written by Jerry B. Jenkins and Tim LaHaye and published by Tyndale, is based on the fundamentalist theology of dispensationalism.

since my birth. I consider him a bona fide saint. His family loved my father as if he were a son.

Yet the strict, fundamentalist form of faith that surrounded my grandfather while he was battling alcoholism didn't offer him much help. At the time, Alcoholics Anonymous was just hitting the scene, in large part because the church hadn't learned how to help addicts.

From what I can surmise, the form of faith my grandfather rejected may have been heavy on finger pointing and light on burden lifting. No one sat me down to explain this; it's simply my best reconstruction from bits and pieces of family lore. This left my grandfather much to react against, which I'm guessing he passed on to his son, who in turn, I'm quite sure, passed it on to me. I have a visceral and angry reaction against any faith that starts to look moralistic or overly rule based.

AS YOU CONSIDER THESE FOUR QUADRANTS OF CHRISTIANITY, YOU MIGHT USE THEM TO BETTER UNDERSTAND THE IMPRESSIONS OF CHRISTIANITY THAT YOU INHERITED BY VIRTUE OF YOUR UPBRINGING.

I note this reaction with irony, because in my early years as a Christian, I slipped into just that kind of religious practice. The Jesus Movement was free-form but vigorous Christianity. I was quite sure I knew better than the establishment-honoring, institutionally ossified faith of my Episcopal upbringing. For all its attention to liturgical detail, to my way of thinking it was a weak-kneed faith that was getting soft in the head.

Adolescents who get religion slip easily into moral superiority.

I was no exception. I had a binary faith—in my perspective, I was either "on" or "off." The rules for holy living; the roles for men and women; the right way of thinking, feeling, and acting in nearly every situation were easy to discern and to be embraced with certainty. There's much about those early years of faith that I treasure. There's also plenty over which I cringe.

So I've been shaped by both influences—my mother's quiet Episcopalian faith and my father's identification as a religious outsider, simultaneously drawn to the vigorous faith of his forefathers and put off by its shortcomings. I've absorbed and reacted against each of these influences. Pilgrims always start somewhere, and that place travels with them wherever they go.

As you consider these four quadrants of Christianity, you might use them to better understand the impressions of Christianity that you inherited by virtue of your upbringing. It's the first step in discerning which direction might take you one step closer to knowing Jesus of Nazareth better.

WHAT YOU'VE ADDED ALONG THE WAY

Moving from what you started with, you can now trace your own spiritual pilgrimage, such as it is, through this landscape. Mine involved forays into at least three of the quadrants. Starting off in the liturgical quadrant (the Episcopal Church of the Redeemer just north of Detroit), I fancied myself an atheist after reading the works of Ayn Rand as a fourteen-year-old. This took me off the landscape for awhile, but it didn't erase my history there.

After getting married shortly after high school graduation for the reason most people get married before planning to (let the reader understand), my wife and I found ourselves in great duress as parents who had plenty of growing up to do. We responded to the love and witness of a young couple who were considered "Jesus People," rooted loosely in the evangelical quadrant. I can remember my dismay shortly after coming to faith at seeing the *Time* magazine cover in June 1971 with a Peter Max drawing of Jesus to depict the Jesus People movement. I had no intention of joining a movement—thought I was one of an elite handful of people discovering Jesus for the first time.

One of our earliest mentors in faith was a graduate student at the University of Michigan who grew up in India as a member of the Ceylon Pentecostal Mission. Living in Ann Arbor at the time, we eventually developed close ties to a Christian community that was predominantly Roman Catholic and a center for what became the Catholic charismatic renewal, a form of Pentecostal influence on Catholicism. Later, we became active in a new church movement called Vineyard, which is known for blending influences from the Pentecostal and evangelical quadrants.[16] Ours is the only church in the Vineyard association of churches whose pastor at one point received a blessing with the laying on of hands by then bishop, now Cardinal Cordes, a personal assistant at the time to His Holiness John Paul II. My next-door neighbor is Ralph Martin, one of the leading lay Catholic evangelists in the world. Sometimes I feel like a very minor Forrest Gump in the Christian landscape. Perhaps you can see why the image of pilgrimage resonates with me.

---

16. See Rich Nathan and Ken Wilson, Empowered Evangelicals: Bringing Together the Best of the Evangelical and Charismatic Worlds (Ampelon Publishing, 2008).

NEW CONNECTIONS RESHAPING THE LANDSCAPE

As you can see from this whirlwind tour, there is a trend in the process of reshaping Christianity in the twenty-first century. From the perspective of this graphic, it could be called *border blending*. It looks something like this:

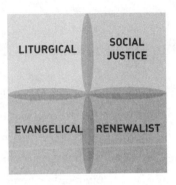

Wherever you look these days, there is blending going on.[17] People from liturgical traditions are influenced by charismatics, who are influenced by Pentecostals. Evangelicals are discovering fixed-hour prayer, a practice of monastic communities in the liturgical portion of the quadrant. Younger evangelicals often contend that rampant abortion and sexual promiscuity are not the only social evils; AIDS, poverty, and care for the environment are moral issues too.

The swirl of influences can be invigorating and sometimes dizzying. Many African American churches have blended social justice with

---

17. If this graphic were three-dimensional, it could represent the extent of border blending much better, because it seems to involve every possible combination.

evangelical and charismatic sensibilities. Churches that have never blended these before are now doing so. My friend James Rhodenhiser, rector of St. Clare of Assisi Episcopal Church (a liturgical church with a long history of social justice concern), began his pastorate there by dancing charismatically at his ordination and then launching a first-ever Bible study program that drew eighty eager participants for serious weekly Bible study. The times are definitely changing.

CORNER DWELLING CONTINUES

Not that there aren't corner dwellers in this landscape . . . Corner dwellers are those convinced that their camp has an exclusive understanding of the truth and merits the God-awarded corner on the market. Within the liturgical quadrant, you can find those who believe that church unity will happen only when everyone returns to headquarters as the binding authority of faith and practice. Within the evangelical quadrant are plenty of people who see unity as a simple matter of adopting their literal reading of the Bible, which is patently, obviously, and unassailably correct in all its particulars. And so on and so forth.

LITURGICAL	SOCIAL JUSTICE
EVANGELICAL	RENEWALIST

In the old days, we were all corner dwellers because we lived and did our religion in cultural-intellectual-geographic ghettos, unaware of any other approaches. In my neighborhood growing up, you knew who the Catholics were because they were a minority, and you didn't attend their church because your clergyperson warned you against such things. I've met Catholics on the East Coast who tell me they only knew of Protestants by reputation.

But mass media, increased mobility, loosening social ties, and a more cooperative attitude have broken that down. Enter the Internet. Now, to be a corner dweller, you really have to work at it; you have to intentionally create and sustain a group-think ethos through social control mechanisms, contempt for others, and a defensive mentality. Even then, your child is only a mouse click away from the rest of the world.

THE TUG TOWARD THE CENTER

The thrust of history, and, I believe, the dynamic of the Spirit, is not toward the corners but toward the interior borders and, ultimately, toward the center. The center is the heart of the matter, the matter being God as understood and experienced and revealed by Jesus.

As pilgrims scattered throughout this landscape take one step closer to knowing, one step closer to the center, new connections are taking place between people; new information is being exchanged; new expressions of faith are emerging.

The center is not a lowest-common-denominator spirituality. It is a recombinant spirituality that is yearning, growing, moving toward a new synthesis or, more likely, several versions of a new synthesis, converging toward a center that has always been there but is rarely occupied.

The conviction that one quadrant or the other owns the trademark on the truth is disintegrating as it encounters the hard rock of reality. The move toward the center is often a step from a pilgrim's point of origin in one quadrant toward treasures located in higher concentrations in a neighboring quadrant. There's much to be learned by the curious, open-minded, and discerning traveler in this landscape.

Different aspects of the *active* dimension of Jesus brand spirituality can be found in the social justice, evangelical, and renewalist quadrants. The social justice quadrant encourages social activism aimed at changing social structures. Nevertheless, the evangelical and renewalist quadrants, focused more heavily on personal piety, have historically fueled major social movements like the abolition of slavery. The kind of change that spreads from person to person until a tipping point is reached is often fueled in these quadrants.

Many of the *contemplative* treasures of faith are imbedded in the liturgical quadrant, especially in the monastic tradition. At first glance, the liturgical emphasis on set prayers and ritual seems a far cry from the experiential delights of the renewalist quadrant. Dig a little deeper, though, and you find some wild-eyed mystics in those monasteries having dreams and visions and ecstasies that are not far removed from Pentecostalism.

The *biblical* treasures, long emphasized in the evangelical quadrant, are finding fresh expressions in other quadrants as evangelical and Pentecostal scholars gain greater acceptance across tribal boundaries.[18] Perhaps the most influential scholar in the field of historical Jesus studies is the Anglican bishop N. T. Wright, who is highly regarded by many younger evangelicals.

The *communal* treasures find different expressions throughout this landscape. The social justice quadrant is inspired by the search for a beloved community of racial and inclusive harmony. The liturgical quadrant has a profound love for the historical church enterprise and its emphasis on "the communion of saints." The evangelical and renewalist quadrants tend to emphasize personal gatherings of pilgrims in small groups.

Discovering how these treasures will affect one another as they interact in new ways is the reason you want to be around for all this.

The center is packed with tribal treasures, but it holds more loosely to tribal loyalties. The center is and always has been a place beyond all places. The center is not ultimately Rome or Geneva or Canterbury or Constantinople, not Azusa Street or Colorado Springs.[19] Nor is it even Jerusalem.[20] The journey home is from and through these and other places, wherever it is we find ourselves.

The center makes of every place a way station. It's the center toward which Abraham was drawn when he left Ur for a place the

---

18. Examples include Ben Witherington III, a noted Jesus scholar who is also an evangelical, and Gordon Fee, a noted New Testament scholar who is also a Pentecostal. Viroslav Wolf from Yale Divinity School (not a Pentecostal institution) has roots in the Pentecostal movement in Romania.

19. The centers of Roman Catholicism, the Protestant Reformation, the Anglican tradition, Eastern Orthodoxy, Pentecostalism, and American evangelicalism, respectively.

20. The center of Judaism and Christianity and one of the centers of Islam.

Lord would show him. The center is the place he looked forward to, "the city . . . whose builder and maker is God" (Heb. 11:10 NKJV).

The center, if such exists, is a place we cannot find but is finding us . . . a city where the streets have no name, whose memory, tucked away in all our hearts, makes of every other place the "not yet" place, because a pilgrim is one who says, "I still haven't found what I'm looking for."

JESUS BRAND SPIRITUALITY STUDY QUESTIONS: ORIENTATION TO THE LANDSCAPE

If you are discussing these questions in a group, you may want to refer to the Discussion Ground Rules for guidance. These can be found in the appendix.

1. What are some of the impressions you have of Christianity in contemporary society that exemplify what the author refers to as "trademark infringement on the Jesus brand" [see p. 6]?

2. Are you (or do you have a loved one who is) reluctant to pursue spirituality on the Jesus path because of negative associations with the religion that bears his name? How do you see those associations affecting you (or your loved one)?

3. How do you feel about viewing spirituality as a pilgrimage focused on taking the next step closer God? What are the advantages (and perhaps disadvantages) of this approach [see pp. 4–7]?

4. Trace some of the influences that have shaped your view of faith, using either the big picture quadrant of world religions [see p. 19] or the quadrant of Christianity [see p. 24].

5. What are some of your observations, thoughts, or experiences of what the author describe as "border blending" [pp. 31–32] or "corner dwelling" [see pp. 32–33].

6. What are some of your observations, thoughts, or experiences of what the author describes as "the tug toward the center" [see pp. 33–36].

ACTIVE DIMENSION

3
REPAIRING THE WORLD

I had a painful epiphany a couple of years ago. I had been invited to a retreat hosted by the Harvard Center for Health and the Global Environment and the National Association of Evangelicals. The participants included thirteen of the top environmental scientists of our time, including E. O. Wilson, a world-famous biologist, and Jim Hansen, a NASA expert on climate change. Mixing it up with them were fourteen religious leaders like myself, though most were academics, unlike myself. We were to discover together our common ground: concern for the earth—the bewitched, bothered, and bewildered earth, that is—suffering a growing environmental crisis.

I was deeply moved by the scientists' missionary zeal to protect the environment. They had a message of alarm and hope. Many of them felt a mystical connection with the subject of their study. Their concern extended across a broad horizon, such as the threat to earth's vast biodiversity and the effects of global climate change, with the poor in underdeveloped nations bound to suffer more than the rest of us if current trends continue. They perceived these conditions as a moral crisis calling for a vigorous change of heart and will.

Yet many of the scientists assembled claimed no religious commitment, preferring to describe themselves as "secular," which means "of this world." They tiptoed around God-talk as though handling a newly discovered radioisotope. Nevertheless, out of love for the world, they agreed to speak again of nature as "the creation," a decidedly unsecular term. Why? To reach out to my community, the faith community, the community claiming to represent Jesus, who was God's gift to the world for love of the world. Because we somehow had become the part of the population most resistant to their concerns for the world.

There's a 1990 movie that didn't make much of a splash at the box office, but it made a big impression on me. It was called *Flatliners,* the improbable story of medical students who induce cardiac arrest in each other (one at a time) to effect near-death experience. During these temporary death spells, these students are disturbed by visions of regretful acts they had committed. Sitting there at the retreat, I had a little version of that.

I saw the rolled eyes of faith comrades (not those at the retreat) at the shenanigans of the "tree huggers," the knowing glances exchanged in response to the "environmental wackos." I saw myself mirroring this shameful posture at times. I felt the subtle contempt, the feeling of moral superiority aimed at "secular" science and, when my little flashback was over, I kid you not, I felt the wrath of God in the form of tribal shame—shame on behalf of my religious tribe, that is.

This is an example of trademark infringement on the Jesus brand. Religious contempt toward those who care passionately about the environment has nothing to do with Jesus, but it has found a way into much of the religion that bears his name. I hope and pray this is changing, but when an environmental scientist encounters contempt, the scientist often assumes the contemptuous person also carries the name Christian. Some of this is media stereotyping. But I mix and mingle with a lot of Christians, and I can tell you it's not just a stereotype.

Too many people who claim loyalty to Jesus have been taking their cues from voices on the radio or cable television, voices of self-professed "news entertainers." All someone has to do is wrap himself in the flag and build a powerful enough media platform, and we hang on every word he speaks as though it were the gospel. Often, the media is just feeding us a party line that may or may not have anything to do with Jesus.

RELIGIOUS CONTEMPT TOWARD THOSE WHO CARE PASSIONATELY ABOUT THE ENVIRONMENT HAS NOTHING TO DO WITH JESUS. BUT IT HAS FOUND A WAY INTO MUCH OF THE RELIGION THAT BEARS HIS NAME.

In time this too shall pass—is passing, I trust— and the most prominent mixed loyalties will be of another sort. But in the meantime, we have to look out for trademark infringement wherever it occurs.

This would be a good time to think of Jesus as the attractor buried in the messy field of religion. Since religion can both illuminate and obscure Jesus, sometimes we need to dig to find him. A good place to dig is the Gospels. Here we find Jesus on a mission from God to repair the world. In his glance, we catch an invitation for us to join him.

JUSTICE FOR THE OPPRESSED

After an extended period of solitude in the Judean wilderness, Jesus returned with the clarity and conviction that only the desert can bring. Like the prophets of old, he had wrestled with God and heard his voice, and the words of God burned within him. Jesus went into the north country of Israel, a nation under Roman occupation; he went to the region he knew well, having grown up there.

> SINCE RELIGION CAN BOTH ILLUMINATE AND OBSCURE JESUS, SOMETIMES WE NEED TO DIG TO FIND HIM.

He came to Nazareth, his hometown. Nazareth is close to Sepphoris, where it's likely Jesus and his father, Joseph, worked as carpenters on the theaters and entertainment centers built there by the Roman occupiers. We know that in Nazareth, a large number of Jewish insurrectionists were crucified by the Roman occupation force, their corpses left hanging by the side of the road leading out of town. This took place when Jesus would have been a child.

Jesus entered his hometown synagogue on the Sabbath and was honored by an invitation to read from the sacred Torah scroll.

Unrolling it, his eyes fell on the words of the prophet Isaiah, which he read to all assembled:

> "The Spirit of the Lord is on me,
>> because he has anointed me
>> to proclaim good news to the poor.
> He has sent me to proclaim freedom for the prisoners
>> and recovery of sight for the blind,
> to set the oppressed free,
>> to proclaim the year of the Lord's favor."
> (Luke 4:18–19)

He then sat down, taking the posture of the teaching rabbi, and announced, "Today this scripture is fulfilled in your hearing" (v. 21).

This is the seminal address of Jesus' public ministry, containing the seeds of all that would follow. It functioned as an inaugural address as well, for the beginning of his reign was at hand. The application, of course, was original, but the language was not. Jesus was using the justice motif of the Hebrew prophets to frame his message and mission. Good news for the poor. Freedom for the prisoners. Release for the oppressed.[1] The beginning of the year of Jubilee, when all debts accumulated by those who couldn't bear them were to be canceled.[2]

Jesus was intending to right wrongs and to deal with the

---

1. The sacred text that informed Jesus always understands poverty in the light of oppression. For example, Psalm 12:5 says, "Because the needy are oppressed and the poor cry out in misery, I will rise up and give them the help they long for" (The Book of Common Prayer).

2. Bible scholars believe "the year of the Lord's favor" in Luke 4:19 is a reference to the Jubilee, a practice referenced in the law of Moses calling for the canceling of debts every fiftieth year, though there is no evidence that it was ever practiced in ancient Israel, making Jesus' announcement even more significant.

oppressive powers-that-be so the downtrodden of this world could be lifted up. This would be better for all of us, because things would be as they were meant to be if God were in charge. Jesus was intending to exercise God's authority in ways it hadn't been exercised before. He was making what can only be understood as a power move.

When Jesus went from village to village declaring, "Repent, for the kingdom of heaven is at hand (Matt. 4:17 NKJV)," he wasn't just talking about the need for individuals to clean up their moral act. He was speaking, like the prophets before him, to the nation as a whole: *repent, turn from your current course as a nation, and recognize God's authority now at work in your midst.* He was reshaping Israel's national agenda.[3]

Jesus began to do something that would have been perceived as a threat to the vested powers of the day. He gathered the poor and oppressed in large crowds and announced their new empowerment: *blessed are you; the kingdom is yours for the taking* (see Matt. 5:3). What all this meant wasn't immediately clear. His disciples were hard-pressed to keep up with him, let alone fully grasp his message. The Roman overlords kept a cautious eye on him through the religious leadership who served at their pleasure. Those in the power centers of the nation sent observers to question him and report back. Jesus was making a lot of people nervous.

But the people who were getting a raw deal from the current system delighted in him. Whoever he was, they knew he was on their side.

---

3. For an expansion on this perspective see N. T. Wright, *The Challenge of Jesus* (London: SPCK, 2000).

In the ancient world, it was understood that the powers-that-be had a spiritual as well as a this-worldly aspect.[4] Rome was in power because the Roman gods were a force to contend with. Israel's lack of political standing wasn't just a disgrace to national pride; it was a shameful reflection on Israel's God. When Jesus went about healing the sick and exorcising people caught in the grip of demonic powers, people didn't think of him as a religious showboater performing onstage to gather the gullible; they saw him as a person of authority tangling with the powers that influenced powers-that-be. Whatever Jesus was up to, everyone understood that he was a force to contend with.

WHATEVER JESUS WAS UP TO, EVERYONE UNDERSTOOD THAT HE WAS A FORCE TO CONTEND WITH.

How did Jesus exercise this authority of his, and to what end? To the end of helping people, empowering the disenfranchised, healing the sick, bringing relief to the tormented, feeding the hungry—to the end of showing Israel a different and better way to be Israel.[5] How was Israel supposed to respond to the Roman occupation? What was Israel's role in the world? The healing and empowering deeds of Jesus were all very personal, but the movement he was generating—the crowds, the message spreading through the nation, the speculation about

---

4. For an understanding of the worldly aspect of the biblical view of the powers-that-be, see Walter Wink, *The Powers That Be: Theology for a New Millennium* (New York: Galilee Trade, 1999). For an understanding of the spiritual aspect of the biblical view, see Charles Kraft, *Christianity with Power: Your Worldview and Your Experience with the Supernatural* (Eugene, OR: Wipf and Stock, 2005).

5. See N. T. Wright's *The Challenge of Jesus* (London: SPCK, 2000) for an understanding of the message of Jesus in historical context.

where it was all headed—had a much bigger feel than a charismatic self-improvement guru coming to a local large venue for a weekend of religious entertainment.

Several years ago, my wife and I were just getting to know another young couple. Brian was a professional engineer who was being treated for a psychiatric disorder, which was well managed with medication. His wife, Angie, was a fun-loving, idealistic social worker with a passion for helping people in need.

Horribly, Angie was shot and killed in her own home by her husband, Brian. Making sense of a senseless act is a fool's errand, but in the days immediately following her death, it became known that Angie's husband had become delusional. He had been laid off from his job at a small engineering firm and had lost his health insurance. He stopped taking his medication and quickly deteriorated. He became mental, unbalanced, fearing that he and his wife would become homeless, and in a confused state, inexplicably, he shot his wife while she lay napping. He made no effort to cover up the crime and, when he realized what he'd done, felt the most profound remorse for it.

We used to sing a song at church that troubled me. Every time we sang it, I thought of Brian and Angie. The refrain of the song went, "God is in control." I understand that there is a long tradition in the Jesus movement that accepts this as a given, but to my way of thinking, God was not yet in full control when Angie's husband killed her.

At best, God is still in the process of gaining control, but until we all learn to cooperate with him a little more, it's not quite accomplished yet. Whether or not it's inevitable is another question, but it's certainly not a fully realized present condition.

Jesus said, "The kingdom of God is at hand" (Mark 1:15 NKJV).

At hand. On the way. Coming. In some sense here, but not quite yet. He will bring it, but we all have a part to play in its arrival. We're to get with the program so the kingdom may come, so his will may be done on earth as it is in heaven.

What would it take for Jesus to redress the wrong done to Angie and to all those who mourn her, to make up for all the ways the world will not be the place it might have been if she had been here longer? We know that forgiveness is of high value to Jesus. Jesus extends God's forgiveness to sinners. Saul of Tarsus, who later became known as St. Paul, with intention, planning, malice, and in possession of a sound mind, participated in the murder of an early disciple of Jesus. Paul was forgiven. But forgiveness and mercy extended to Angie's distraught husband is only part of what needs to happen to right this wrong.

Jesus brings a kind of justice that cares about the broad social issues contributing to a person on the edge losing his equilibrium. I worked as a registered nurse in the field of community mental health and know that some psychiatric medications should not be abruptly discontinued. Something is wrong when people in a nation surrounded with good health care don't have access to it. (To say nothing of the unavailability of even the most basic health care in other parts of the world.) That's a wrong that needs to be righted. Inspired by Jesus, we could lend a hand to that effort. I have a friend, Linc, whose nonprofit company is working to find solutions for a health-care system in the United States that leaves millions of people uninsured. He and his company are doing the Lord's work. We should talk to the Lincs of this world and find out how we can help.

The religion of Jesus put a premium on caring for the most vulnerable among us as the sign of authentic religious practice (see James

1:27).[6] In the New Testament era, the paradigmatic group of the most vulnerable among us was "the widows and the orphans." It's not too great a stretch to think that the "widows and orphans" of our day include single moms and their families, raised without the help of husbands and fathers. Inspired by Jesus, we who are men could do everything in our power to stay connected with our children and the mothers of our children. Societal structures that make this more difficult could be wisely adjusted. In the meantime, communities of faith promoting the cause of Jesus could help him exercise more control in the world by creatively caring for single moms and their families, leveraging the resources of the community to do so.

My wife, Nancy, leads a ministry in our church to offer support to single moms and their families. We host a moms' night out once a month during which we care for and feed the children of the single moms while serving the moms a gourmet dinner. Not lousy church potluck fare, but a meal prepared by skilled chefs and served by uniformed wait staff. Our goal is to make the moms feel pampered so they are encouraged in their difficult task. The evening facilitates relationships that further support the moms. Other support also flows from that base, including a car repair ministry. Caring for the most vulnerable isn't a matter of compassion alone; it's a demand of justice and the sign of true religion.

Well and good. But now the hard part: Angie herself. What can be done to right the wrong done to her? I take comfort in the hope that Angie's disembodied spirit is being comforted in the arms of a loving God in heaven. But that doesn't satisfy my longing for jus-

---

6. Intriguingly, this letter may have been written by James, the brother of Jesus and leader of the church In Jerusalem. Its tone certainly resonates with the timbre of Jesus' prophetic voice.

tice for Angie. Something was lost to Angie that needs to be restored, and until it is restored, justice will not have been done. Angie needs her vivacious, pulsating, material-spiritual human-in-the-image-of-God-on-God's-good-earth life back.

This is where the empty tomb of Jesus comes in, for without it, there is no ultimate justice for Angie. The canonical Gospels and the movement from which they emerged bear witness that Jesus of Nazareth, crucified, dead, and buried, rose again on the third day into a transformed material-spiritual, human-in-the-image-of-God existence that prefigures a new creation to come.[7] Admittedly, this is a wildly audacious hope, but it is the hope that fueled the movement that led to our having a conversation about Jesus in the first place. If it's a vain hope, so is the hope that "the arc of the moral universe is long, but it bends toward justice."[8]

You will have to decide for yourself whether this is a hope worth holding on to. It took time for the earliest disciples to overcome the shock of it enough to make sense of it and to understand its significance. We're granted the same space to poke and prod before coming to our own conclusions.

The case against resurrection is the sheer improbability of such

---

7. One could think of this as analogous to a "phase change," as when water at a certain atmospheric pressure and temperature suddenly undergoes a phase change from liquid to gaseous form. (For more on this analogy, see John Polkinghorne, *Quarks, Chaos, and Christianity* [New York: Crossroad, 1994], 82–83.) The resurrection body of Jesus is understood in the New Testament as in some sense continuous with his body before death and in another sense discontinuous with that body, in the way that a plant is continuous and discontinuous with the seed from which it springs forth. All this is implied in the phrase "a transformed material-spiritual existence."

8. A favorite quote of the Reverend Dr. Martin Luther King Jr., famously used in his "God Is Marching On!" speech, March 21, 1965, Montgomery. Full text available at http://www.stanford.edu/group/King/publications/speeches/Our_God_is_marching_on.html (accessed October 23, 2007).

a thing ever happening. But one also has to consider the improbabilities on the other side. The early disciples of Jesus were shown to be normal, fear-ridden individuals. How did they find the courage to proclaim a risen Savior if the sealed tomb wasn't found to be empty with Jesus appearing more or less as the Gospels describe it?

The later, so-called Gnostic gospels, such as the recently discovered *Gospel of Judas*, take the path of least resistance: Jesus lives on in purely spiritual, disembodied existence, just as the Greeks taught we all will. Not exactly a faith to turn the world upside down.[9] How does that fit with the audacious, earthy, provocative Jesus who is such an arresting figure in the Gospels? What's the gut-wrenching drama in a Jesus who dies a martyr's death and then simply lives on in collective memory? *Something* got this powerful movement started that continues today despite all our efforts to undermine it.[10]

In the end, we can read the accounts that lie closest to the events in question, asking ourselves whether they bear the ring of truth. We can explore, consider, open our hearts (without shutting down our minds), and maybe even ask for some help from God to understand—and then proceed accordingly.

So yes, there are things to believe or not about Jesus. But the primary context for faith to emerge isn't a class on Christian doctrine taught by an expert. The context is an active engagement with the world in need of repair.

As pilgrims drawn to the center, we can take one step closer to

---

9. For the most exhaustive case for the resurrection of Jesus argued from the standpoint of historical evidence, see N. T. Wright, *The Resurrection of the Son of God* (Minneapolis: Augsburg Fortress, 2003).

10. I refer to the misguided efforts of practitioners, not skeptics.

knowing Jesus by listening to his teaching on God's coming reign of justice and finding needs around us to which we can lend a hand, informed by his perspective. As we engage with the realities that engaged Jesus' attention, we're more likely to encounter him.

BREAKING THE CYCLE OF VIOLENCE

My oceanographer friend, the one who describes himself as secular in outlook, was able to see through all the off-putting distractions of what passes for Christianity to understand that Jesus introduced the counterintuitive notion of loving one's enemies. He describes this as facilitating what he has come to understand through the science of biology—that all life is related.[11] This is why he counts Charles Darwin and Jesus as his two heros.

You got that right, Doctor. Jesus wants us to love our enemies (Luke 6:27, 35). Not only this, but one could also say that the entire Jesus movement is to be organized around love of enemies. Jesus is the expression of God's love for all of us who have opposed, through the failings of our lives and perspectives, the coming of God's kingdom here on earth as it is in heaven. Jesus taught us only to expect God's forgiveness inasmuch as we are willing to extend it toward those who trespass

AS WE ENGAGE WITH THE REALITIES THAT ENGAGED JESUS' ATTENTION, WE'RE MORE LIKELY TO ENCOUNTER HIM.

---

11. See Carl Safina, "Something New Under the Sun," www.expedition.com.

against us (Matt. 6:12).[12] And Jesus advised Israel that their approach to Roman occupation—violent resistance—would lead to destruction unless they began to practice love of enemies.[13]

The message Jesus brings is meant to be like a stone dropped in a pond that causes a ripple effect.[14] The transformation begins in our hearts, affects our relationships, and extends outward to address our most pressing global concerns. The gospel is a message with a personal, social, and global reach. If it's not good news at all these levels, it's not good enough.

THE GOSPEL IS A MESSAGE WITH A PERSONAL, SOCIAL, AND GLOBAL REACH. IF IT'S NOT GOOD NEWS AT ALL THESE LEVELS, IT'S NOT GOOD ENOUGH.

On the personal level, what marriage can long survive, or failing that, what divorced couple can cooperate in the care of their children, without the power of forgiveness rooted in love for those who harm us? How do we overcome the poison of hatred at work in our own souls without learning to love our enemies? How do we reconcile within ourselves the wrongs done to us by others absent the power of this message?

On the social level, Mohandas Gandhi led a nonviolent resistance

---

12. This would include, if not define, our enemies.

13. This is the import of Jesus' teaching in the Sermon on the Mount to "turn the other cheek" (Matt. 5:39) and "walk the extra mile" (Matt. 5:41). Both of these would have been understood as a counterintuitive response to Roman occupation.

14. I'm indebted to Tri Robinson and Jason Chatraw, coauthors of *Saving God's Green Earth: Rediscovering the Church's Responsibility for Environmental Stewardship* (Norcross, GA: Ampelon, 2006), for this image.

movement to overthrow the occupation of India by the British army; he was inspired by the teaching of Jesus in the gospel of Matthew regarding love of enemies, the power of turning the other cheek, and going the extra mile.

Dr. Martin Luther King Jr., inspired by the success of Gandhi, implemented a similar strategy to overcome the evil of structurally imbedded racism in the United States. The African American churches of the time were the foundation for this movement. Is it a mere accident of history that both leaders lost their lives by assassination, as did the one who inspired their deeds?

On the global level, as we watch the Middle East conflict spill over into a form of tribal warfare that threatens every nation on earth, can we afford to ignore the message of Jesus to learn how to love our enemies before it's too late?

Could we learn from the example of the Truth and Reconciliation Commission's work in South Africa after the overthrow of apartheid?[15] Led by Archbishop Desmond Tutu, the commission came up with a way to respond to the evil of apartheid. Those who committed crimes during this era were invited to receive pardon, but only after public acknowledgment of the wrongs done and willingness to face the victims of their crimes. This approach is credited with breaking the cycle of violence in that country.

What if the followers of Jesus in the United States called a unilateral end to the so-called culture wars pitting people of faith against "secular humanists"? It seems that many people of faith consider it a religious duty to bare their fangs in response to those with whom

---

15. See Desmond Tutu, *No Future without Forgiveness: A Personal Overview of South Africa's Truth and Reconciliation Commission* (New York: Random House, 2000).

they disagree, forgetting that each time they do, they distance themselves from the God they are seeking to defend.

Consider this modest proposal: Christians who object to the teaching of evolution in the public schools could observe a one-year moratorium on attempts to overturn the teaching of evolution in the schools; the effort expended would then be directed toward volunteering to help public school science teachers with any classroom needs they might have. When the year of service is over, Christian leaders with concerns about evolution could gather with leaders in the field of evolutionary science simply to understand each other's conflicting perspectives. Their aim would not be to debate the issue, but to grow in understanding of the other side's view. Once each side was able to accurately restate the other side's views, tentative explorations of common ground could be undertaken.[16]

WHAT IF THE FOLLOWERS OF JESUS IN THE UNITED STATES CALLED A UNILATERAL END TO THE SO-CALLED CULTURE WARS PITTING PEOPLE OF FAITH AGAINST "SECULAR HUMANISTS"?

The Monty Python movie *Life of Brian* includes a scene in which Jesus is preaching, but his voice is too faint to be heard at the back of the crowd.[17] He says, "Blessed are the peacemakers." Some older women are heard to be saying, "What'd

---

16. As part of this yearlong suspension of hostilities, people of faith would boycott any media voices who use contempt toward those with whom they disagree, as a kind of "love your enemy" fast.

17. I'm grateful to Carl Safina for pointing out this scene to me.

he say? I can't hear 'im very well." A younger person answers solemnly, "He said, 'Blessed are the cheese makers.'" This sets off a round of, "Why is he saying that? What's so special about those people? Why is he playing favorites?" Perhaps it's time we all got a little closer and listened to what Jesus is really saying.

TENDING THE GARDEN

One of the greatest global threats we face is the growing environmental crisis: air and water pollution, ecosystem collapse in developing countries, an alarming increase in the extinction rate of animals and plants (and with the latter, the loss of potentially disease-curing drugs), and the threats associated with climate change. Because the poor are less protected from the vagaries of the natural environment, they are especially vulnerable to the harm caused by environmental degradation. The environmental crisis, therefore, is a matter of acute concern to the God whose heart is especially tender toward the poor.

Judging from his many citations, Jesus was fond of the book of Genesis, first among the books in the Hebrew Bible. One of his sayings harkened back to Genesis: "From the beginning, it was not so." In the gospel of John, the resurrection account harkens back to the Genesis garden and forward to a new creation. Jesus appears near the empty tomb early in the morning on the first day of a new week. Mary Magdalene encounters him and mistakes him for the gardener. This is John's way of emphasizing the resurrection as the beginning of a new creation.

Jesus isn't just about helping us get to heaven when we die. He didn't teach us to pray, "Get us out of this mess on earth and let us into heaven!" The destiny of the disembodied soul after death is at best a minor theme in the New Testament writings, which focus instead on God's kingdom coming to earth. Jesus said, "When you pray, say . . . Your will be done on earth as it is in heaven" (Luke 11:2 NKJV). Jesus is about the *renewal* of the earth, which has already begun. Those who follow him are to act as though the earth is the Lord's, because it is.

> JESUS IS ABOUT THE *RENEWAL* OF THE EARTH, WHICH HAS ALREADY BEGUN. THOSE WHO FOLLOW HIM ARE TO ACT AS THOUGH THE EARTH IS THE LORD'S, BECAUSE IT IS.

There are plenty of reasons rooted in self-interest and power politics and the powers-that-be to keep us from not caring about the earth as though it were the Lord's. Much in our society leads us to treat the earth as a disposable resource, caring little that we are using it up for future generations.

Here in the United States, we use quite a bit more than our fair share of energy. We account for much more than our fair share of carbon dioxide released into the atmosphere from the burning of fossil fuels; these emissions are known to be an important factor in the climate's warming, leading to harmful effects for centuries to come because a large percentage of the carbon remains in the atmosphere for hundreds of years. The fuel we burn also pollutes the air we breathe and the water we drink. The coal we burn to generate electricity releases mercury into the atmosphere, which gets into the food chain so that pregnant women who eat too much fish endanger the health of their unborn children. Asthma rates are on the rise, especially in our urban centers, among the most vulnerable.

These are wrongs that need righting, problems in our world that need fixing. The message of Jesus addresses these concerns if we have ears to hear. These are complex problems that can only be solved by extraordinary cooperation—cooperation on a scale never before required of humanity. We need good science to help fix the problems created by the technologies we adopted without counting the cost of their adoption. We need action by individuals and governments and cooperative actions among nations. We need wisdom. We need help.

We can't get there from here without a shared concern for justice, rooted in the hope of a better world. We can't get there from here without learning to get along across political, cultural, social, religious, and geographic divides. We can't get there from here without a substantially increased capacity to practice love, including love of our enemies and those with whom we don't easily get along. Jesus could be a source of leadership and inspiration as we tackle these problems together.

At the retreat I attended with those scientists regarding the environment, James Gustave Speth, the dean of the Yale School of Forestry and Environmental Studies, the first scientific adviser to the U.S. president on climate change, stood up and said, "I used to think if we threw enough good science at the environmental problems, we could solve them. I was wrong. The main threats to the environment are not biodiversity loss, pollution, and climate change, as I thought once. They are selfishness and greed and pride. And for that we need a spiritual and cultural transformation, something we scientists don't know much about. Maybe it's time for us scientists, including those of us who are not religious, to work together with people of faith to help that along."

Or as Jesus would say, "Repent, believe the good news. The kingdom is at hand."

4

HEALING ALONG THE WAY

My father had a favorite word: *bass-ackwards*. Sometimes I wonder if those of us who promote the religion of Jesus have gotten something bass-ackwards. Have we front-loaded people with so many matters of belief that we are, in effect, asking them to swallow the whole package as a prerequisite for meaningful engagement with Jesus?

A young man came to our church with his wife and kids. He wasn't a practicing anything at the time. He found himself moved during the services, tears inexplicably falling down his face, that sort of thing. We met a time or two and talked about his experiences and what they might mean. He found himself being drawn to Jesus, and he responded.

Then he came to our membership class. During the membership class it was suggested to him (by me) that he read our church bylaws, which include a standard twelve-point statement of faith. Some of the points in that statement of faith were hard for him to swallow. I told him that he didn't have to swallow them all in order to respond to Jesus, but I'm not sure this registered. During the class, he decided to respond to Jesus by getting baptized. His baptism was the last time I saw him at church for quite a while.

You can't crawl into another person's soul and know what's going on in there. But after being in the pastor business for so many years, I've developed a kind of intuition I've learned to listen to. My intuition tells me it wasn't helpful for this young man to read our statement of faith as the threshold for authentic Christianity. I think it gave him the impression that he was expected to swallow the thing whole or not at all, and unless and until he did, he had no business thinking of himself as a Christian. It's making me rethink how we use something like a statement of faith.

Have we forgotten that the Christian doctrinal system has been in development for more than two thousand years, rooted in ways of thinking that are even older? The tradition-bound Judaism of Jesus' time was a younger, less-developed system than Christianity is today. Is it possible that our current rendering of the Jesus faith has gotten so developed as to be unwieldy? Its sheer weight is certainly intimidating. The doctrinal formulations are often written in language designed to address controversies that are no longer pressing concerns, using thought forms that are now remote or moot.[1]

The first-generation disciples were actively engaged with Jesus before they fully understood that he was making messianic claims or what those claims meant. Compared to people considering the Christian truth claims today, the disciples had a lot more breathing

---

1. For example, the doctrine called "transubstantiation" (that the wine of Communion becomes the blood of Christ) is based on Aristotelian understanding of physics, which makes a distinction between the "substance" of a thing and its "accidents." This is a philosophical distinction that we simply don't use anymore.

room, a lot more latitude of perspective within which to engage Jesus. It isn't until halfway through the gospel of Mark that Jesus turns to Peter and says, "Who do you say I am?" (8:29)—and even then, Jesus asks this without any veiled threat to disown Peter if he got the answer wrong.

BELIEVING

I didn't come to faith by accepting a statement of faith summarizing doctrinal perspectives that were more than four hundred years in the making.[2] In fact, the first time I saw a statement of faith, it said that God created some people to be the elect and others he created to be the damned.[3] I handed that statement of faith back to the pastor who gave it to me and said, "Even if this were true, I think it would be wrong to teach it."

I wasn't even aware that statements of faith were part of the process of coming to faith when I first started. Maybe this was the core gift, the treasure of the Jesus Movement, the religious movement of the late 1960s that provided me with the cultural context for engagement with Jesus. (If you want a feel for it, listen to "Slow Train Coming" by Bob Dylan, who made his own start toward Jesus as a part of this movement.)

---

2. The Christian understanding of God as a Trinity of coequal "persons" took that long to develop into the form articulated in the Nicene Creed; other perspectives in even the simplest summaries of faith took longer to develop in the form represented in the statements. The earliest confession of faith was simply, "Jesus is Lord"—and there were no doubt those who hastened to add, "properly understood."

3. This particular statement of faith was called the Canons of Dort.

I had been to confirmation class as a kid.[4] I memorized the Ten Commandments and the Apostle's Creed and the longer Nicene Creed.[5] The class influenced and informed me, but at the time it didn't take. I got hung up on a question that I never bothered to ask in class: *Why would God want to be praised? Is he some kind of egomaniac?* I couldn't swallow the package, and I didn't feel that questioning the package was allowed. After confirmation, I stopped going to church.

Several years later, I read the gospel of Matthew in a weak moment. My fascination with Jesus had begun, and reading the Bible only made it worse. I was *impressed* by the Jesus portrayed in Matthew. I found myself annoyed by some of his teaching, but overall his message was attractive. *He* was attractive.

At a certain point I came to a decision: *I need to pursue this now, while I have the chance.* I realized that if I didn't take another step closer to knowing, I might never take a step closer to knowing, because I was fully capable of ignoring this growing fascination. I could replace it with another fascination. But somewhere in my gut, I felt that if I did so, it would end up on my list of deathbed regrets. Maybe top of the list. The thought haunted me, not because I imagined myself afraid to die without faith, but because I wanted to avoid that painful sense of an opportunity missed.

That Jesus may have risen from the dead seemed plausible to me. Just that—plausible. I didn't know how such a thing could be verified. I couldn't imagine an experiment to demonstrate it. It just

---

4. A class at my Episcopal church designed to teach young people about the core beliefs of the Christian faith.

5. These are beautiful statements of faith from the second and fourth centuries, respectively.

seemed that whatever wonder the world is an expression of could plausibly be thought to be capable of such a thing.

I didn't have any opinions about whether the Bible was the Word of God and, if so, in what sense. I didn't have any opinions about whether Jesus was born of a virgin. I didn't have any opinions about the existence of or the nature of heaven and hell or whether Jesus was the only way a person could connect with God. I had impressions from the teaching of Jesus in the Gospels about these things, but they were sketchy. I wasn't always sure how he was using terms and what exactly he meant by things he said touching on these topics.

The package that drew me wasn't the system of Christian doctrine. The package was the person, Jesus. And thankfully, thankfully, thankfully—and for this reason alone I will always love them; this book is dedicated to them—the people around me who were on their own path toward the center thought that was just fine. I didn't feel any pressure from them to swallow any faith package whole. I just felt a sense of shared excitement with them about taking one step closer to knowing.

So I offered myself to Jesus as a disciple, a student, a follower. I was young and thought I was pretty hot stuff. I imagined that Jesus, should he in fact exist as I was hoping he did, enough to follow at least, would be pleased by this new addition to his group of followers.

If you had interrupted me in the act of offering myself to say, "Ken, do you know that you are a sinner?" I would have said something like, "A sinner? I guess so. Isn't everyone?" If you pressed further to ask, "Do you believe that Jesus died to save you from your sins?" I would have said something like, "I don't know. How does that *work*?"

Biologists tell us that when baby ducklings first open their eyes and see their mother duck hovering above them, something happens in their brains called imprinting, and from that moment on they know that they too are ducks. For better or worse, this early experience imprinted something on my brain: taking that step toward Jesus, without swallowing any package whole, is what I cannot but believe is the heart of the matter. All the other explanations of how things work, to call into service the nearby metaphor, roll off like water on a duck's back.

We're drawn to Jesus. We respond. And things happen along the way to confirm, or expand, or cause us to ask other questions or face other dilemmas, and we see if we're drawn and we see if we respond. I realize I cannot formulate this into a doctrine that can be taught in seminary, but it's how I think it really works.

The only stuff that happens, happens *along the way*. Get going and see what happens.

HEART MENDING

The Reverend Dr. Martin Luther King Jr. faced a crisis of faith early on in the civil rights movement. He was living in Birmingham, Alabama, and found himself leading the church-based bus boycott that began when Rosa Parks refused to give up her seat at the front of the bus. Dr. King was the new minister in town, and leading the boycott fell to him by a kind of accident. He was at the wrong place at the wrong time and became the leader.

In this case, becoming the leader of the bus boycott meant becoming the target of death threats. His phone number wasn't yet unlisted, so hateful people called him at night threatening to blow up his house with his family in it if he didn't call off the boycott.

Alone at the kitchen table one of these horrible nights after one of these horrible calls, Dr. King had to decide what to do. His biographers tell us that Dr. King's form of Christian faith at the time wasn't so much a matter of personal trust—Dr. King trusted Jesus to help him and lead him in the personal way that many people speak of today. His faith was a kind of philosophical understanding shaped by the Christian ethic.[6] But at the kitchen table that night, he had some tough decisions to make, and he didn't know how to make them.

Head in hands, Dr. King presented his dilemma to God: the people were looking to him as a leader, but he was filled with fear, at the end of his own strength, unable to continue. Slumped over the kitchen table, he suddenly felt what he called "the presence of the Divine" as these words resonated within: "Stand up for justice, stand up for truth; and God will be at your side forever."[7] His fears "almost at once" subsided. He had what he needed.

As we take steps toward the center, toward the fulfillment of the longings of our pilgrimage, things happen to us along the way. Things happen to us that convince us of needs we didn't know we had; things unfold between us and the divine that we may not even be seeking until we hit a particular point along the path.

---

6. For example, the title of King's doctoral dissertation was "A Comparison of the Conception of God in the Thinking of Paul Tillich and Henry Nelson Wieman." See Charles Marsh, *The Beloved Community: How Faith Shapes Social Justice, from the Civil Rights Movement to Today* (New York: Basic, 2006).

7. Martin Luther King Jr., *Stride Toward Freedom* (New York: Harper, 1987).

The year my fascination with Jesus really kicked into gear, I was a sophomore at the University of Michigan, married, the father of a young child, and working whenever and wherever I could. I got a part-time work-study job, funded by the university, at the local community mental health center. I was pretty good at helping people in crisis, so I was asked if I wanted to be trained as a suicide prevention worker to staff the suicide prevention hotline.

One night while I was at home "on call," trying to sleep in the living room near the phone, hoping no one would be thinking about suicide that night or dialing the hotline that would patch the call in to my apartment, the phone rang. It was a young veteran back from Vietnam, calling from a phone booth in the parking lot of a bar. He told me that he had ingested an overdose of barbiturates and just wanted to tell another human being why he did it, before losing consciousness. There was no way in those days to trace the call. All I could do was try to keep him on the line in the hopes of gaining his confidence enough to learn where he might be to send him help.

I was nineteen years old at the time and feeling out of my depth. The man's voice began to slur, and I knew he was slipping away. Before he did, I asked his permission to share about my new-found understanding of Jesus as a sign to all of us that God knows, loves, and cares about us, no matter how bad things get. With permission, I prayed with him over the phone. Eventually the conversation just ended. I never knew what happened to the man.

When the call was over, I got mad. Mad at myself for not having anything else to do but talk and pray. Mad at the community mental health center for letting a neophyte like me staff the suicide prevention phone. But most of all, mad at God for putting me in the position of being possibly the last person on earth to talk to this troubled soul. *What do you think you're doing putting me in a spot like that?*

Something was happening to me along the way. I went to talk to my favorite pastor, Dick Bieber. His church in inner-city Detroit seemed like the kind of place Jesus would have enjoyed. Drunks from the infamous Cass Corridor would come to church stinking of alcohol, and people loved and accepted them. Professors from nearby Wayne State University and businesspeople who drove in from the suburbs to hear Dick preach would mix it up with street people and irreverent Jesus freaks wearing their OshKosh overalls to church.

I told Dick how mad I was at God for putting me in that tight spot with so little to give, and he just smiled. Then he told me a story that Jesus told of a man who went to his ornery neighbor at midnight because guests had just arrived and the man had nothing in his cupboards to feed them. The neighbor fussed and fumed, but he eventually handed over some bread so the man who had the late-arriving guests could give them something to eat (Luke 11:5–8).

I got it. I was the man whose cupboards were empty when someone late at night needed something I didn't have to give. God was the ornery neighbor who gave me some bread just to get me off the porch. My job was to pester God for what I needed, whether I thought God felt like giving it to me or not.

"So what is it," I asked Dick, "that I need to go out and get?" He asked me what I thought it was. I said, "I think it's more of a God connection than I feel right now. I think it's more of the Holy Spirit. Jesus talked about the Holy Spirit like someone we feel close to, but I don't really know what he's talking about."

"Do you want more of the Holy Spirit, then?" Dick asked.

"Yes," I said. "Come back on Wednesday night," he told me, "and after the Bible study we'll gather around and help you ask for more of the Holy Spirit."

It can't be that easy, I thought. But I trusted Dick and knew that he knew of what he spoke, so I came back nervous but hopeful.

After the Bible study was over on Wednesday evening, Dick invited me to come to the front, where he and a few others would pray with me to help ask for what I wanted more of. Man, was I nervous. This seemed very much like a situation where something spiritual was supposed to happen, and I wasn't sure I was in the mood. I was sure I couldn't make anything spiritual happen. I hoped these people wouldn't be disappointed when what they asked for didn't occur.

Dick served us Communion, then he suggested I kneel while the others gathered around for the laying on of hands, and quietly some prayers took place. I was kneeling there worried about the fact that nothing was going to happen, wondering whether I even believed in a Holy Spirit after all—Jesus I liked, but who was the Holy Spirit? To get myself out of this mental wormhole, I decided to cheat and pray the Lord's Prayer, for lack of anything else to pray.

I hadn't prayed the Lord's Prayer in years. I used to pray this prayer in my bed as a kind of magical incantation to ward off things that hide in the shadows in a child's room. As a brand-new and much more sophisticated disciple of Jesus, I wasn't inclined to pray this kids' prayer. Except that I did, there and then.

Our Father . . . For the first time, the thought dawned on me: *God is offering to be my dad. He's willing to be my dad. I want him to be my dad.* Only it was a little more personal than that. Like, *I'm your dad now and will be forever.* I suddenly felt very lucky. My throat tightened with that burning sensation young men have when they are fighting back tears. I couldn't finish my prayer. I was stuck on the father part.

You've got to understand: I was a dad myself then, but I was far from feeling up to the task. I wasn't used to feeling over my head in need. I was in the stage of human development when people need to feel a growing sense of mastery. I was feeling just the opposite.

I'm your dad now and will be forever sounds like something you might read in a cheesy greeting card. But it did not sound like that to me. It felt like a dream where you're at the place where the aliens have just landed and they come out of their spacecraft and with the most believable kindness say, "Peace, all shall be well; your planet is safe forever."

No, I didn't feel electricity shoot through my body, like some people I know. I don't know what the people around me saw or felt. I just know something happened. Or something began to unfold that night that is unfolding still. Some little epiphany sparked a growing awareness that, looking back, hasn't left me. I think that was the missing bread in my cupboard.

These kinds of things, or other kinds of things that fit you better than they fit me, happen *along the way*. The sequence of these things isn't set in stone. Nothing necessarily has to come first. It's not so clear as many people make it out to be that these three things in this order are the necessary three things in that order.

Yes, certain themes recur. Willingness to surrender when you reach the point where surrender is called for. Willingness to trust when trustworthiness has been sufficiently demonstrated. Willingness to do what you are told to do when it's clear that the one doing the telling is God.

But how all this works itself out can't be captured in a formula.

It's the makings of the story that you and God are writing together and will be for the rest of your life.

As you take a step closer to knowing the Jesus who is repairing the world, it's helpful to understand that this is part of an ongoing story that involves you. Among other things, it's a mending story. He's about repairing the world, and he invites you to help him get the job done. And while that's under way, things are meant to happen that mend you.

WE ARE PART OF AN ENORMOUSLY COMPLEX SYSTEM OF CONNECTIONS, A NETWORK IN WHICH THE SLIGHTEST CHANGES AT ANY ONE PART MAY HAVE A CASCADING EFFECT THAT TOUCHES THE WHOLE.

I'm trying to stay far away from that debate about whether the world as a whole needs to be fixed before we as individuals are, or whether we need to be fixed one at a time before the world can improve. That's one of those old meaningless debates like, "Which came first, the chicken or the egg"?[8] We are part of an enormously complex system of connections, a network in which the slightest changes at any one part may have a cascading effect that touches the whole. We change, and the network changes. The network changes, and we change along with it. Repairing the world, and the mending of each of us in it, is all of a piece with the work of God involving us.

The mending happens to us in so many ways along the way. Our

---

8. It's a meaningless debate, because a population of birds, through a gradual process of adaptation to changing environments, over a very long period time, became what we call chickens today. They and their eggs did, that is.

fears are allayed as they were for Dr. King that night when he laid his head on the kitchen table and prayed. Our bodies are constantly in the process of mending, or we'd all die in short order. Our care and tending of each other through medicine and love and prayer and many other means mends us. Sometimes the mending just allows us to let go and die in peace; other times it causes us to snap out of it and prevail. Sometimes the mending is tender and gentle. At other times it feels brutal, as when we're enabled to survive or even move on despite unspeakable horrors. There's a *lot* of mending that needs to be done.

BODY MENDING

The Jesus of the Gospels was actively engaged in healing the sick. He did it a lot, but it was scattershot. That is, it didn't seem to be part of an overall public health strategy to increase longevity. People in a given locale begged him to stay longer and do more, and he shook his head no and moved on to the next village to get his message of the coming kingdom of justice out.

Jesus is compassion driven. His message doesn't seem to be about him as much as about the sick people getting better. Jesus never told stories about how he healed people in the previous town in order to rev people up in the next town about his message. From the stories included in the Gospels, he got phenomenal results. Even the most skeptical scholars, including those who think many of the miracles in the Gospels didn't happen, seem to acknowledge that Jesus healed people.[9]

---

9. Marcus Borg, *Jesus: A New Vision* (San Francisco: HarperSanFrancisco, 1991), 61.

This might make you nervous, but Jesus also told *us* to heal people. By "us," I mean people who are curious enough about him to want to learn more. In fact, the first-generation disciples were sent out to heal the sick before they had arrived at any conclusions about Jesus being the promised Messiah.[10] *Go heal people.* Hmm . . . talk about a deal breaker. But what does that mean? You might think it means you have to make like the sweaty, fleshy preachers on television holding the microphone, talking to gullible people, and pushing them over to the cheers of the crowd. And you're thinking, *No thanks.* Me too.

What if it just means, "Go heal people?" What if it means, "Don't shy away from the sick and the outcast?" (If you've ever been really sick, you know how isolating an experience it is.) Instead, draw near to them, as Jesus did when he shocked the leper by touching him because he was "moved with compassion" (Mark 1:41 NKJV). This phrase, in the original language, Greek, means "moved in the bowels," thought to be the seat of emotion. Now we know that long nerves from the brain go straight to the gut where some emotions are felt. So the ancients weren't quite as dumb as we think they were.

Go heal people. It's not about showing off. It's not about proving how profoundly wonderful you are. It's about repairing people's broken bodies because God made himself a world and loves it. How can you do such a thing? Do what you can, not what you can't. Stop their bleeding, clean their wounds, and see that they get the medical

---

10. The term *Messiah* refers to an individual, longed for by Israel, who would come to make things right, and especially to deliver them from foreign occupation.

care they need, like the good Samaritan in the story Jesus told about the poor man mugged on the road and left there half dead (Luke 10:25–37).

Be willing to go out on another kind of limb as the situation warrants. If people are willing, try to heal them as Jesus did. At least try. With permission, place a hand on their shoulder, open your eyes and your heart toward the wonder that the world is an expression of, and slip into that space that Jesus occupied, where God was known as Abba, Father. And then, like Jesus did, do as you are moved to do or instructed on the spot to do. Say to the pain, "Stop." Or to the body, "Be healed."

Don't make a show of it if you get a little success. Don't tell stories that make you look like the healing hero. Some friends brought a man with a speech and hearing problem (they often go together) to Jesus so he could heal the man. Jesus pulled him away from all the gawkers to tend to him more privately (Mark 7:31–37). Wouldn't it be great, just once, if the people who did healing on television (and I've been around long enough to think some of that healing really happens, though much of it doesn't as it appears) turned to the camera and said, "This is not a show; point the camera somewhere else. Actually, what are we doing on television, anyway?"

Shortly after I came to faith, my father landed in an intensive care unit in a deep coma, his body impervious to pain, and his kidneys having shut down. After days in a coma, the doctors warned us that even if he came out of the coma, he would likely be severely disabled. It was pretty grim.

A friend and I went to the chapel and prayed for my dad. We were hoping the tide would turn. While we were in there praying, Dick Bieber, the pastor I mentioned earlier, was visiting my dad. He had been talking with my dad about the new fascination with Jesus my dad had been experiencing in a very dark time in his life.

Dick was talking to my dad, who was lying there in a deep coma. He was saying things like, "Glen, you are loved by God and a lot of people. Wake up; there's hope."

As Dick turned to leave, the nurse in the unit told him, "Pastor, Mr. Wilson is in a very deep coma and can't hear you." Dick knew that, of course, but he graciously said something like, "Thanks for letting me know."

At that point, my dad spoke up and said, "Thanks for coming, Dick." This provoked some surprised reassessment of his condition. Obviously, he was waking up. And more wondrously, he kept waking up until soon he was just fine. He had to go through intensive physical therapy to loosen a shoulder that lost range of motion as he lay there not moving for days. And he had to go through intense counseling to deal with some things that respond to counseling. But in time, he was just fine.

You never know what's going on. Was it just a happy coincidence or divine intervention? Hard to tell.

My sister and my mother were in the unit the next morning, though, and overheard the doctors on their rounds commenting on my father's case the way they sometimes do as if no one else is listening. They said, "It's the closest thing to witchcraft we've ever seen."

Since then, I became more open-minded about the possibility that the words *go heal people* are words from Jesus worth paying closer attention to. Do what you can, not what you can't. But sometimes you can do more than what you think you can if you are willing to go out on a limb and try.

The frustrating part to me is this: I know healing is possible. I've seen it work. After thirty-five-plus years of trying and watching others try and hearing reports of credible witnesses, I know it works. It just doesn't work as much as I think it's needed or as much as I want it to work.

As I write this, a dear friend is in the nearby hospital in a coma, having undergone a very serious medical emergency that almost killed her. There she lies, still alive, but just barely. *To what end?* I'm thinking. I've visited her many times, spoken to her words I hoped God would use to wake her up. Hopeful words, because I know it can happen. But it hasn't happened. None of this makes sense to me.

I know people who believe in healing have explanations. Many of the explanations have to do with how much faith I have or she has, or whether I'm using the right words, or whether I'm using the right words with the right theology behind them, or whether I'm plugged in enough to get results. That last part makes sense to me. I don't think I'm plugged in enough to get the results Jesus seems to have gotten. As I said, it's frustrating.

But so what? It's not about me. Some of the most effective healers in the world, whether by means of prayer or complicated surgeries or medical interventions, are also the most frustrated people, because things don't work as well as they want them to and the sick people need them to. One of the most effective faith healers was Aimee Semple McPherson.[11] People crowded around Aimee every time she came to town, and wonderful things happened that showed up in the newspapers, written by skeptical reporters who were as surprised as

---

11. *Sister Aimee: The Life of Aimee Semple McPherson* by Daniel Mark Epstein (New York: Harcourt Brace Jovanovich, 1993) is the best book about her and details the extraordinary results she achieved. This book was not written by an adoring follower of McPherson.

that nurse in the intensive care unit was when my dad said, "Thanks for coming, Dick." Even Aimee got frustrated, though.

I do know that I hear a lot more credible-to-me reports of this kind of healing in places where there are fewer opportunities for the other kind of healing—for example, in places in the developing world where the message of Jesus is moving through a given culture for the first time in history. There are such places.

FAIR DOESN'T SEEM TO BE WHAT HEALING IS ABOUT. IT SEEMS TO BE MORE ABOUT MYSTERY.

That doesn't lessen my frustration, because if you're sick in spite of the best efforts of modern medicine to make you better, your need is as great as someone who is in one of those developing nations where the message of Jesus has been previously unheardof. Fair doesn't seem to be what healing is about. It seems to be more about mystery.

There are plenty of reasons not to try, but I think we should try. Because sick people who don't have other options need us to try. We should do what we can, not what we can't, and we should also be open to doing things we think we can't, because maybe we can.

A single woman, pregnant with twins, came to our church out of sheer desperation. Her previous religious affiliation had nothing to do with Christianity, but she needed friends and had a high school acquaintance who came to our church. The doctors told her the babies had twin-to-twin transfusion syndrome, which means there was a shared blood supply between the twins when there shouldn't have been. It's very serious, because it usually dooms one or both of the twins, as best I understand.

This young woman came to a small group that my wife leads for single moms. (My wife, by the way, gets better results healing than I do. If I were you and sick, I'd go to her, because I'd feel my chances were somewhat better.) The women in the group found out she had this medical problem that has no known medical solution—all the doctors could do was monitor the situation—and they prayed with her. Not just once or twice, but every time they had the chance and she was willing, which was often.

The woman began to get better reports from the doctors. They told her things were going much better than expected. The twins still had the condition, but it wasn't having the usual effect. As time went on, the doctors were more excited. They asked for her permission to share her case in a special-cases forum for doctors, because it was *very* special.

Eventually, the twins were born prematurely, as many twins are, but both babies were healthy. I'm so happy for her and the twins, but I'm still bothered that healing like that doesn't happen more often. If I'm a student of Jesus, though, I'm only expected to keep learning.

I have my share of pet theories concerning why we don't get better results than we do, but they are just that, theories; until they are tested, there's no sense bothering you with them.[12]

One thing keeps me living in the tension between the occasional inexplicable healing and the too-frequent lack of intended results. Jesus spoke of the reign of God as coming in two different ways. Sometimes he spoke as if this coming reign were already here,

---

12. I wish other people who had pet theories would find a way to test them before foisting them on the rest of us.

I THINK WE'RE ALL SUPPOSED TO LONG FOR MORE OF THE "NOT YET" TO BECOME THE "ALREADY."

or at least near at hand, like your next breath. At other times he spoke of this coming reign as coming, in the sense of "not yet here." So this tension that I live in is at least a tension that Jesus seems to recognize in general between the "already" of what he's up to and the "not yet" of what's to come. Having made the distinction, I think we're all supposed to long for more of the "not yet" to become the "already."

SOUL MENDING

We often think of the soul as something apart from the body, but the tradition that informed Jesus didn't see it that way. In his tradition, the Hebrew tradition, the soul is more like an expression of the person in his or her wholeness. As the creation story in Genesis 2 tells us, God breathed into Adam, and Adam became a living soul (v. 7). Another way to say it is that we are enfleshed spirits and inspirited flesh. We are soul.

I think addictions might be best described as a disease of the soul in this sense. There's something very physical going on in addictions. Genetic predisposition probably plays a role; it's certainly the case that some addictions are physiologically much harder to beat than others. Let's hope for a medical breakthrough that will help. But addictions also seem to respond positively to what we think of as spiritual interventions.

Why wouldn't they, if we are soul?

As a pastor, I talk to a lot of people suffering from addictions. I see firsthand how much pain in the world is fueled by addictions. In fact, if there were one way to improve the world so that significant social problems would be greatly lessened and the world itself would change for the better, it would be to mend the soul by curing addictions. Apart from the classic addictions—to alcohol, drugs, gambling, and the like—sin itself seems to have an addictive quality.

I think Jesus, the treasure buried in the field of religion (Matt. 13:44–46), is the source of a great deal of soul mending when it comes to addictions.

A recent study by researchers at the University of Michigan Addiction Research Center indicates that measures of spirituality tend to increase during alcohol recovery.[13] Those who experience an increase in day-to-day spiritual experiences and sense of purpose in life are more likely to sustain recovery. The study indicated that these results did not depend on participation in Alcoholics Anonymous. (Alcoholics Anonymous is the most well-known and widespread approach to treating alcoholism with a spiritual program.)

I would be surprised if Jesus brand spirituality were the only form of spirituality that had this effect. I'm not aware of any study demonstrating that it is. But I do think that the demonstrated impact of spirituality on recovery from alcohol addiction says something important about Jesus brand spirituality—just not over and against other spiritualities.

It's a fact of history that the recovery principles of Alcoholics Anonymous, summarized in the twelve steps, were distilled from

---

13. Elizabeth Robinson, PhD, Kirk Brouwer, MD, James Cranford, PhD, and John Webb, PhD, "Six-Month Changes in Spirituality, Religiousness, and Heavy Drinking in Treatment-Seeking Sample," *Journal of Studies on Alcohol and Drugs,* 68, no. 2 (March 2007) 282–90.

Christian spirituality. What became AA was first associated with something called the Oxford Group, a form of evangelical Christian faith.

People bandy about the word *prophetic* nearly as much as the word *journey*. But I think the story of Alcoholics Anonymous is a story through which God is speaking and, in that sense, prophetic.

You may know that Bill Wilson, the cofounder of AA, was an end-stage alcoholic whose recovery began when a friend of his who had gotten a Jesus brand form of religion started talking to him about the power of religion to change lives. Bill Wilson's physician, unable to successfully treat Bill's alcoholism, told him that a religious conversion sometimes helped. He didn't know how to lead his patient toward one other than to advise him to get one. In the hospital, drying out from yet another binge, Bill Wilson got one.

In the depths of his torment, Wilson issued the unknowable challenge: "If there be a God, let Him show Himself now!" he shouted. As if in response to his demand, the room suddenly filled with light. It was bright and white, a benign, enveloping presence that seemed more than a match for the terror he had been feeling just moments before. Then he saw himself on a mountaintop, with a wind blowing toward him. The wind moved closer and closer, then through him. Then the man who had been bound up in a seemingly irresolvable struggle felt profoundly free.[14]

---

14. Francis Hartigan, *Bill W.: A Biography of Alcoholics Anonymous Cofounder Bill Wilson* (New York: Thomas Dunne, 2000), 61.

The context for this experience was Bill's connection with the Oxford Group. These are the people he approached to help him sustain the new freedom he gained from using alcohol. The principles he integrated into the twelve steps were principles he learned from people who derived them from the message of Jesus.

You'd be wrong to think this is a story of Christian triumphalism. Perhaps Bill Wilson realized that his principles of recovery couldn't be practiced as plainly as they needed to be practiced inside the camp of Christianity. The culture of the church in general at that time wasn't a good one for recovering alcoholics. It was too focused on applying moral effort to stop the sinful drinking, and it didn't work. One biographer indicates that Bill Wilson didn't view drinking as a sin, as his Oxford Group fellows did, and that many of his other views were outside the accepted views of these dedicated Christians as well.[15]

So Bill Wilson, as aware as he was of the connection between those twelve steps and the religion of Jesus, made a decision to take AA outside the camp of Christianity. This strategy included the counsel to entrust one's life to "a Power greater than ourselves."[16] This wording annoys many Christians. They would much prefer that Jesus be named the official higher power. In fact there's been a long history of something like sibling rivalry between AA and the church, though in recent decades both parties are getting along much better.

Perhaps Jesus is more interested in helping drunks get better than in getting the credit. If your brain is pickled in alcohol it's difficult to follow any path, let alone the Jesus path.

---

15. See Hartigan's discussion in *Bill W.*, especially p. 68.

16. "The Twelve Steps of Alcoholics Anonymous," step 2, http://www.alcoholicsanonymous.org/en_information_aa.cfm?PageID=17&SubPage=68. (accessed October 23, 2007).

I think God sent Alcoholics Anonymous outside the camp of the church with his blessing on each one of those twelve steps, his presence hovering wherever two or three alcoholics bent on recovery gathered. Through AA, God was both helping as many alcoholics as would have his help and slapping the church in the face to wake them up. In large part, it's worked. The church today is a much healthier environment than it used to be for recovering alcoholics. Many churches sponsor their own recovery programs, and the spirituality of the twelve steps has found its way back into the camp.

I think this is a lesson for the church: we shouldn't just look for God to show up inside our camp; we should look for him to show up outside our camp as well. Jesus, after all, went outside the camp to do his most important work.

JESUS BRAND SPIRITUALITY STUDY QUESTIONS: ACTIVE DIMENSION

If you are discussing these questions in a group, you may want to refer to the Discussion Ground Rules for guidance. These can be found in the appendix.

1. The author depicts contempt as incompatible with Jesus Brand Spirituality [see pp. 41–44]. What are some experiences you've had on the giving and the receiving side of contempt over matters of spirituality or religion?

2. What do you think of the author's view that a concern for justice is at the heart of Jesus' message? Does this differ from your impression or understanding of the Christian message?

3. Why do you think care for the environment is consistent or inconsistent with the teaching of Jesus?

4. The author describes coming to a point of eagerness to follow Jesus without understanding or accepting doctrinal formulations that many would consider essential for authentic faith [see pp. 61–66.] What do you think of this? Is it possible to be a disciple of Jesus while remaining unsettled about what many consider core issues of faith?

5. The author describes an experience of awakening to a sense of God's nearness as a father [see pp. 68–73]. Have you ever felt a sense of God's nearness, and if so, what was it like?

6. If you or someone you know has experienced help from a twelve-step recovery program and wish to share about it, how did it affect your/their understanding of spirituality?

CONTEMPLATIVE DIMENSION

5
MYSTICALLY WIRED

For centuries, we've specialized in breaking things down to manageable units to aid our understanding—the body into separate systems, matter into its constituent parts, successful relationships into ten quality characteristics. We've ground things into a pretty fine dust to measure and weigh and otherwise examine; but the magic, the mystery, the wonder of life is found in the connections. We're better at taking things apart than putting them back together.

For too long, the active and the contemplative dimensions of spirituality have been viewed in isolation from each other, distorting both. Practitioners have tended to specialize in one or the other. But Jesus combined both in his own person. He was an activist, a man with a message on a mission, working to make the world a better place. But he was also a contemplative with an inner life marked by a deep awareness of God that connected him with others and all living things.

"Very early in the morning, while it was still dark, Jesus got up,

JESUS BRAND SPIRITUALITY CONNECTS US TO GOD, ONE ANOTHER, AND ALL LIVING THINGS.

left the house and went off to a solitary place, where he prayed" (Mark 1:35). This wasn't the beginning of a day of retreat from the world, but a day of active engagement as Jesus traveled to villages throughout Galilee, spreading his message and resisting evil.

Jesus brand spirituality connects us to God, one another, and all living things. The emotive aspects of that connection—the warm, loving, and powerful feelings that often come with faith—are designed to move us to action on behalf of God, one another, and all living things.

REGAINING OUR BEARINGS ON SPIRITUAL EXPERIENCE

When it comes to spiritual experience, we in the developed Western world have been through a centuries-long wasteland. The recent explosion of interest in all things spiritual—whether the fad over angels, or the varied New Age practices, or kabbalah (a form of Jewish mysticism), or the Pentecostal and charismatic movements within Christianity—is a kind of early gasping for air, as if we've been holding our breath for too long.

This underdeveloped understanding of spiritual experience can be traced to our forefathers, who toyed with the notion that we are all just complicated machines—thinking brains influencing doing bodies. The tendency to reduce things to their parts is characteristic of a convergence of factors that created the modern era, including the advent of rationalism and the scientific method. Where does that leave the mystery of existence itself? The founding philosopher of the modern era, René Descartes, began with a first principle: "I think therefore I am." He viewed the body as a machine, often guided by a nonmaterial mind. "I think therefore I am" was never intended to tell the whole story of who we are. We could also say, "I sing therefore I am," or to paraphrase Desmond Tutu, "You are therefore I am." But in time, "I think therefore I am" became the dominant understanding.

As a result of our long and productive love affair with rationalism, we tend to suffer from an anemic view of what we call "spiritual experience." Various Christian movements have sought to restore a legitimate place for spiritual experience, but the options are still limited. The evangelical quadrant is marked by the experience of conversion or new birth, a more or less sudden (but always dynamic) transition that is described in accounts that have a definite before-and-after flavor.[1] The renewalist quadrant is shaped by the experience called "Spirit baptism," marked by the transrational experience of speaking in tongues.

Even within these religious persuasions, many feel conflicted by the topic of spiritual experience. Perhaps you come from an evangelical background, but your story of coming to faith doesn't fit neatly into the before-and-after motif. Maybe you attend a church in the renewalist quadrant, but you don't have the same experiences that are celebrated there, or you have them without the requisite

---

1. Charles Colson, *Born Again* rev. ed. (Grand Rapids: Chosen, 2004). This 1976 best-seller details one such before-and-after conversion experience.

frequency or intensity. You feel as though you'll always be the designated driver.

Perhaps the whole idea of religious experience as portrayed in popular culture or experienced in brief forays into this realm is a complete turnoff and contributes to keeping you on the outside of faith looking in.

Many years ago, I invited my father-in-law, an executive at General Motors, to a charismatic prayer meeting. My father-in-law stood there in a state of utter confusion while two young men behind him prayed loudly in tongues—he would have called it gibberish—for about thirty minutes, and the rest of the crowd was singing and swaying and raising a cacophony of prayer and praise. *What was I thinking, inviting him into this?* I thought. Afterward, bless his heart, my father-in-law was looking for something positive to say before returning home. He put his arm on my shoulder and said, "Ken, I can't say that I understand what the hell you're involved in here, but you sure are raising a great family." It's one of the most powerful compliments I've ever received in my life, but it came at a great cost to my father-in-law!

Let's begin by backing up. Let's understand spiritual experience as something that is part of our humanity.

NEUROSCIENCE SAYS IT'S NORMAL

Neuroscientists are still in the earliest stages of understanding the human brain. Compared to our understanding of other things, our understanding of the brain is primitive. But some things are becoming clear. New research suggests that the human brain seems to be wired for mystical experience.[2] Buddhist monks or Catholic nuns meditating under the watchful eye of brain imaging devices have the same parts of the brain lighting up. Something's really happening, and that something is an important part of what it means to be human. Whether some people are more prone to such experiences than others is unknown, but the parts of the brain lighting up are parts we all have.

Let's assume there's more to the realm of spiritual experience than is represented by our current and rather meager expectations or by what we perceive to be the authorized experiences in a particular religious framework. When it comes to mystical experience, we are just coming out of the Age of Polite Silence.

This has affected everyone, regardless of belief or religious background. The reason we tend to think of spiritual experience as weird is that, until recently, it has been relegated to the fringes of our worldview.

PERCEPTIONS SHAPED BY WORLDVIEW LENSES

Reality is more than we can take in raw; we first have to filter it through our senses. Then we have to make sense of what our senses detect. Enter a worldview. A worldview can be thought of as the lens through which we interpret what we perceive from the world based on our assumptions about reality. We assume that certain categories of phenomena do happen and others don't; these assumptions shape

---

2. See, for example, Andrew Newberg, MD, Eugene D'Aquili, MD, PhD, and Vince Rause, *Why God Won't Go Away* (New York: Ballantine, 2001).

our expectations. As the psychologists have demonstrated in their experiments, our expectations shape our perceptions. This is an important point. We can all see that perceptions shape expectations.

A WORLDVIEW CAN BE THOUGHT OF AS THE LENS THROUGH WHICH WE INTERPRET WHAT WE PERCEIVE FROM THE WORLD BASED ON OUR ASSUMPTIONS ABOUT REALITY.

If we see the sun rise every morning, we expect it to rise this morning. But expectations and assumptions also tend to shape *perceptions*. When the unexpected happens, we tend to have more difficulty perceiving it, or we interpret it with preexisting categories that may or may not be helpful.

Imagine being on the shore of the island called Guanahani, now part of the Bahamas, when Columbus sailed in aboard the *Pinta*. You've never seen a large ocean vessel emerge at the edge of the horizon from parts unknown. Because it's so unexpected and unfamiliar, your mind might play tricks on you before the reality registers. For the same reason, it takes an inordinate amount of time for people to recognize a playing card that has a black heart as anything other than a spade.

Our worldview assumptions are all the more powerful because they remain mostly unexamined. We inherit them from the culture in which we are imbedded, and they are reinforced in multiple ways. In fact, that's one of the primary things a culture does: it reinforces a worldview.

There is no single Christian worldview, no single American worldview, no single twenty-first-century worldview. Instead there is a shifting set of lenses, many of which we share in common with others.

We can have experiences that register only on the far fringes of our worldview. They are not widely regarded as normal; we have only limited language to describe them, so we don't. These remain strictly private experiences with little reinforcement. When this occurs, such experiences may seem weird or dim. They may barely register.

As a result, we find ourselves in a worldview-induced state of confusion regarding spiritual experience. We crave spiritual experience, but it may also bother us because it feels like we're giving in to an appetite for the weird.

In fact, I think it's possible that those who are enamored of certain spiritual experiences may have a tendency to emphasize the culturally unusual aspects of the experience as a way of assuring themselves and others that they are truly spiritual. If your worldview tells you that spiritual experiences are weird, but you also want them badly, you may pursue what is weird as a way of pursuing what is spiritual. So the "weird factor" can cut both ways, putting some people off while causing others to accentuate the weirdness. It's a messy business, religion, especially when we aren't very adept at understanding certain aspects of it.

And yet, for all this, spiritual experiences abound throughout the culture. In a survey conducted in 1975, 35 percent of respondents reported having had spiritual experiences at least once in their life.[3] I have a friend who did a postdoctoral fellowship in cultural anthropology at Harvard and now teaches at a major university.

---

3. See Newberg, D'Aquili, and Rause, *Why God Won't Go Away*, 107.

About ten years ago, he told me of a professional anthropology society that held a workshop that for the first time considered the idea of "spirit" as something more than just a cultural construct. The room was packed because many anthropologists had witnessed some fascinating "spirit phenomena" in field studies around the world; often these phenomena didn't seem to be well explained by the existing categories of cultural anthropology. Even cultural anthropologists view the world through their own worldview lenses.

So spiritual experiences, including contemplative or mystical experiences, haven't had much of a place in our worldview beyond the fringes. But that's changing. As this change continues to unfold, we will eventually get better bearings. All of this won't seem so weird when our worldview shifts to make more room for it. It will happen. Hurry up, I say. I'm tired of thinking of the mysterious dimension of being human as weird instead of beautiful and intriguing and most of all, important.

Let's take a fresh look at the word *contemplative*, for starters, because Jesus was a man of action and contemplation.

CONTEMPLATE FOR A MOMENT

To *contemplate* simply means to look at something thoughtfully and steadily. *Behold.* Your life has been littered with contemplative experiences. The following examples only scratch the surface of the possibilities; they don't even begin to suggest the available categories of experience.

You're out on the ocean. The ocean catches your attention for a brief moment. It seems to be saying, *Take me in.* So you look around, and the busyness of your thoughts, having nothing to do with the ocean, starts to slow down. Or it happens without your paying attention to it. The enormity of the ocean presses in upon you. Your eyes widen, as do your mind and your heart. Time slows because you are absorbed in what lies before you.

Something about the vastness of the ocean seems to be connecting with something inside of you. The world out there and the world in here make a brief connection. As one of the ancient prayers

SPIRITUAL EXPERIENCES, INCLUDING CONTEMPLATIVE OR MYSTICAL EXPERIENCES, HAVEN'T HAD MUCH OF A PLACE IN OUR WORLDVIEW BEYOND THE FRINGES. BUT THAT'S CHANGING.

Jesus would have used says, "Deep calls to deep" (Ps. 42:7).

Or you're heading out to go deer hunting again this year. Your wife says, "I wonder what the appeal is, since you hardly ever bring home a deer." *Ouch.* But as you're driving up north, you ponder that casual, not-intended-to-be-caustic remark. You realize that you just like being there.

You like being out in the woods and having an excuse to sit quietly in the deer stand up in a tree with your cell phone turned off. You like being able to tell yourself, *Be quiet; I'm hunting now,* when your mind acts up and starts reminding you of things left undone. You like it when the feeling of anticipation leads first to impatience (*Hurry up, deer!*) and then into a hopeful calm. You're alert but quiet and still. You're content to be there as long as it takes. Whatever it is feels *good.*

Or you are looking in your toddler's bedroom at night. The moonlight is shining through the window onto your little one's serene face. Your little one who has been a holy terror lately and causing no lack of irritation in you. Only now, all that feels like ancient history. A feeling comes over you that is just that, a feeling; if you had to use words to describe it, they might be, *It's worth it,* or *All shall be well.*

CONTEMPLATION IS ABOUT PERCEIVING CONNECTIONS WITH THE REALITY AROUND US.

Maybe you are at a major league baseball game waiting for something interesting to happen. Or in a concert venue before U2 comes out. Or sitting in a pocket park in Manhattan surrounded by people and tall buildings. All of a sudden . . . no, *sudden* is too strong a word. All of a moment it happens, and every last shred of annoyance you usually feel in crowded conditions evaporates; you feel very closely connected to everyone and everything around you. The moment passes as mysteriously as it came.

It's ironic that we sometimes think that a person in a state of contemplation is "out of it." In fact, contemplation is about perceiving connections with the reality around us. The inner world and the outer world feel connected. When we comtemplate, we feel more connected within ourselves and with others and the world around us.

JESUS WAS APPEALING, NOT WEIRD

However the spirituality of Jesus affected him, it did not make him weird. It didn't disconnect him from the world or the people around him. It made him beautiful and intriguing. It made him appealing, as though by connecting with him we might connect with everything that's beautiful and intriguing about God and ourselves and others and the world around us.

Check out the character of Jesus in the movie *Jesus of Nazareth*, directed by Franco Zefferelli. Yes, it's true; the actor playing Jesus has blue eyes! And he never blinks on camera. It's the director's way of making us think, *There's something different about this guy.* What's different is this: he doesn't meet our expectations for the founder of a world religion. He seems too entirely human for that. Appealingly human. Like that scene in the movie when Levi the tax collector throws a party for his friends, including the rich upper class of fellow tax collectors (considered traitors to the national cause) and their loose women friends. If cocaine had been around in those days, it would have been there at the party.

Levi invites Jesus to the party as the honored guest, and Jesus comes! And what's more, he seems to be having a great time. All those up-and-outers and their loose women seem to really like Jesus because he likes them. They ask him for a little entertainment, which he provides by telling them a story. In the movie, Jesus tells his longest and most involved story, the story of the prodigal son, at this party. "A man had two sons. The younger one said to his father, 'Father give me my share of the inheritance now, because I'm out of here!'" He's got them in the palm of his hands with that story.

Wow, we think. *I would love to be like that when I grow up!*

SEEING BEYOND

When we think of spirituality, our minds immediately go to prayer in its various forms. We may think of contemplative or mystical prayer as being especially spiritual. Then we think about the prayer we've heard from others around the dinner table or prayers that we've prayed ourselves, such as when we're in a real bind and ask God for some help. It seems like "brown paper bag" prayer. It's nothing to crave, per se. Thank God for brown-paper-bag prayers, the ordinary prayers we all do much of the time. Life would be too intense if we couldn't pray that way.

But don't let that fool you or bore you. There's more to prayer than that. Because there's more to *us* than that. We are mystically wired.

We are made or adapted for contact with reality that goes beyond what we think of as ordinary. Call this reality the transcendent dimension—that which goes beyond. By transcendent, I don't necessarily mean something separated from ordinary reality—not separated from the material world, for example, or from the everyday things that happen around us and occupy our attention. I mean something that goes along beside it, is intertwined within it, and goes beyond it.

The God whom Jesus reveals is a transcendent God. He's the God out of whom everything that exists came into being, which ties him very closely to it all; but it also sets him apart from it all, since nothing else is that out of which all things came.

Jesus is about putting us in touch with all of that. All of it: the material world and all the wonder that the material world is an expression of, what is and what transcends what is, including God.

But that's not the whole of prayer. I think of prayer as a catalyst meant to affect our understanding and experience of all of life. So prayer isn't our relationship with God, but it's a powerful catalyst in our relationship with God. Prayer is a catalyst in our relationships with others and with all living things. Prayer affects our interactions and connections with what we call the material world: our work, our play, our science, our engineering, our gardening—everyday and out-of-the-way things—our living, our dying, and whatever happens after that.

PRAYER ISN'T OUR RELATIONSHIP WITH GOD, BUT IT'S A POWERFUL CATALYST IN OUR RELATIONSHIP WITH GOD.

So what does Jesus have to teach us about prayer?

From a certain point of view, not much. Jesus didn't teach a lot *about* prayer. Writers like Henri Nouwen and Thomas Merton have taught a lot more about prayer than Jesus ever did. In the Gospels, we overhear Jesus praying some, especially in the gospel of John. He has a few parables about prayer. And of course, we have the disciples asking Jesus to teach them to pray, in response to which he gives a very brief prayer that we call the Lord's Prayer.

On the whole, Jesus had a rather scattershot approach to teaching us about prayer. I think it's possible Jesus didn't consider that his primary job.

Human beings had been praying long before he came along. Jesus was part of a rich tradition of prayer treated extensively in the Hebrew Scriptures and passed down person to person through the ages. The book of Psalms is the prayer book of the Hebrew Bible, and it's a book Jesus quoted often. The Psalms, for example, provide Jesus with his last words as he died. There are 150 distinct prayers in the book of Psalms, most of them longer than the prayer Jesus taught us to pray.

I think it's possible that Jesus focused more of his energy on revealing to us the God he prayed to, knowing that this, more than anything, would affect our prayers, which would catalyze much more than that.

SEEING THE WORLD AS JESUS DID

To go to the heart of the matter, the contemplative life of Jesus helped him to see the world through the eyes of his Abba, Father. Jesus' favorite and distinctive manner of addressing God was with the Aramaic term *Abba*, a form of "father" that leans in the direction of "papa." I didn't know this at the time, but when I knelt and prayed the Lord's Prayer at the age of nineteen, asking for more of a God connection than I had known and experiencing that eerie but beautiful feeling that God wanted to be my dad, I was having an Abba, Father moment.

We know this is a primary aspect of the spirituality that Jesus meant to pass on to others, because it's right there in the prayer he passed on. "When you pray, say: 'Our Father . . .'" (Luke 11:2 NKJV).

Intimacy is yet another word that's wearing out through overuse. Instead, let's call it closeness. Proximity. The nearness of another.

Abba, Father is about that. We know that Jesus had closeness with God. And this closeness affected the way he perceived and experienced reality.

John the Baptist was out in the Jordan River performing baptisms as a sign that it was time for people to start fresh because God was coming close. Jesus submitted to John's baptism even though John thought Jesus didn't need it. The Gospels say that after Jesus prayed, "Father, glorify your name!" he heard a voice saying, "I have glorified it, and will glorify it again." The bystanders, however, only heard thunder (John 12:28–29). Which was it? It might have been both. As the ancients said it, the heavens opened, it thundered, and in the thunder Jesus heard a voice come to him. We'll never know for sure, but it may not have been the first time. We know it wasn't the last.

Often when Jesus prayed, he sensed the nearness of God by hearing something. Before appointing the twelve apostles as his hand-selected messengers, he spent the night in prayer. Listening. *Which ones, Abba?*

Simon, Andrew . . . We know that when Jesus addressed individuals by name, they sometimes melted. As in the garden on Easter morning when Mary Magdalene saw the Lord and thought at first that he was the gardener. All he had to do was say her name, and she melted. She felt the closeness. Was that because Jesus heard Mary's name spoken by Abba, Father?

Often it seems that Jesus saw things that others couldn't make out as easily. When some of the religious leaders were protesting that his healings on the Sabbath day constituted a violation of God's command, Jesus explained himself by saying, "The Son . . . can do only what he sees his Father doing" (John 5:19). In other words, he

JESUS KEPT HIS EYES OPEN . . . SO THAT HE COULD SEE WHAT THE FATHER WAS DOING AND THEN GO DO IT WITH HIM.

didn't just go around willy-nilly healing people because he had a mind to. Jesus kept his eyes open (the traditional practice of Jewish prayer) so that he could see what the Father was doing and then go do it with him.

It's possible that when Jesus saw the leper and was "moved with compassion" (Mark 1:41 NKJV), he interpreted that movement within his own gut as a sign of Abba, Father's nearness with him and the leper. Perceiving that, he reached out his hand to touch the man and together with Abba, Father, made him better.

It's possible that when Jesus got up before everyone else and left the house and went to a solitary place to pray (Mark 1:35), he wasn't alone. He was *alone with* Abba, Father.

Does this sound appealing?

PRAYER IS A LENS

Think of prayer as analogous to the scientific method. The scientific method is a particular discipline, a particular set of lenses that help us see the world differently by looking at it from another angle. The scientific method isn't just about facts and figures and data and experiments; it's about using those things as a way to change the way we imagine the world. The best scientists are not always the smartest; they are often the most willing to use their imaginations.

A long time ago, we used to think that the material world was made of smaller and smaller pieces of hard matter called particles. Stuff was made up of molecules, which were made up of atoms, which were made up of subatomic particles, like a collection of tiny billiard balls grouped together in the nucleus and circling around it like planets around the sun. That was then; this is now.

Now, through the discipline of the scientific method, through the use of experiments and data and facts and mathematics, scientists imagine the world differently. In fact, there's a growing gap between how scientists perceive the world and how the rest of us do, because they are looking through this lens called the scientific method, which becomes more difficult to see through the thicker it gets. They see the world of physical matter as being foamy and cloudy, popping into and out of existence, impossible to pin down exactly, impossible to predict precisely, mathematical, and almost mystical. Honestly, read something written by the physicists who study matter at the quantum (the micro-mini) level. They sound a little loopy.

The scientific method doesn't just shift your perceptions of reality at a weird or esoteric level—the sort of thing you talk about in your dorm room late at night. It's also about more everyday things.

I saw a public television special on the plight of certain ocean animals. The biologist was explaining that the shark population was in precipitous decline worldwide. How could that be, since the ocean is so huge? How would you even be able to know that the shark population is in decline? You need the scientific method to devise a complicated means to do a shark census. Tag the sharks and track them over time. Count them in certain parts of the ocean and extrapolate from there. Looking through that lens, your perceptions about the world, in this case the shark population, shift.

The scientific method changes perceptions that touch your

heart and make you sad, glad, or mad. On the special about sharks, the biologist pointed out that one of the reasons for the sharp decline in the shark population is the common practice of hauling these impressive animals onto the dock of a boat, slicing their fins off while they are writhing on the deck, and tossing them alive back into the ocean, where they can no longer be seen. It turns out you can make a lot of money from the shark fins. How do people let themselves do such things?

Partly because they don't use their imagination. Once that shark is out of sight, it's out of mind. Maybe when the finless shark goes back into the ocean, it slips away into oblivion. But the narrator said these sharks *drown*. I grew up in the city of Detroit, so I'm not up on my fish. I asked a biologist what it means that a shark can drown. I learned that sharks get their oxygen from the water by swimming through the water. The water runs past their gills, and their gills pull out the oxygen, and they do what we do when we breathe. Ahh! But without their fins, they can't get going. They just move around chaotically in the water. So they can't breathe. And that's how they die down there: gasping for oxygen like we do in one of our drowning nightmares.

So the scientists are seeing the world differently than we are because they are looking through this lens that changes their perceptions. This is why some of them get a little hot under the collar, and when you ask them how they really feel about all this, they sound like one of the Hebrew prophets thundering out denunciations in the name of the Most High.

Prayer, in Jesus brand spirituality, is a lens like that. It helps us to see the world through the eyes of God, understood and experienced as Abba, Father.

6
PRAYER MEANS GOING SOMEWHERE

We live in a time of shifting worldviews, and some of the shifts are making more room for God in our experience. As a result of these changes, the understanding and experience of God that Jesus and his earliest followers had is in the process of becoming more, not less, understandable and accessible to us.

Prayer is about doing something that in some sense allows us to go somewhere. The somewhere that we go is a place where the connections Jesus came to forge—with God, one another, and all living things—are enhanced.

My understanding along with my experience of this began to shift several years ago. I read *The Shaping of a Life*, a memoir by Phyllis Tickle organized around her lifelong experience of prayer.[1] In the memoir, Tickle tells of her childhood impression of her

---

1. Phyllis Tickle, *The Shaping of a Life: A Spiritual Landscape* (Shippensburg, PA: Image, 2003).

mother praying every day at 3:00 p.m. sharp in the living room: that when her mother prayed, she "went somewhere."

In one of her lectures, Tickle refers to the somewhere her mother went as a "nonlocative place." A place. But not "locative," that is, not *located* in the same way that we think of ordinary places being located in our familiar dimensions of space-time.

PRAYER IS ABOUT DOING SOMETHING THAT IN SOME SENSE ALLOWS US TO GO SOMEWHERE.

An example of such a nonlocative place, according to Tickle, is the Internet. We conceive of the Internet as a place, but it's a different kind of place than usual. We "go online" through a portal, our home computer. We travel about on the Internet, visiting various "sites"; when we're done, we "go offline."

For the first time, I had a sensible framework for understanding what was becoming an increasingly frequent experience of prayer, one that felt very much like going somewhere. Though novel to my ears, the Internet analogy made sense. It was as though my mental picture of reality and my experience of reality were finally beginning to integrate. This only served to enhance my experience of prayer.

This understanding of prayer has only recently appeared on our cultural radar screen. Prayer has been traditionally understood and practiced as simply uttering (or thinking) words aimed at God. It certainly is that, but it's much more as well.

Prayer is a way of connecting with God, who is present here and in the realms Jesus referred to as heavenly. The ancients had a worldview that made more room for God in their experience. They operated by a set of assumptions that affected their expectations such that it was easier for them to perceive God nearby. This profoundly shaped their experience of prayer.

To understand new (for us) possibilities in the realm of prayer, we need to think as cultural anthropologists do, comparing the worldview of an ancient people with our own.

A WORLDVIEW WITH MORE ROOM FOR GOD

Dallas Willard, professor of philosophy at the University of Southern California, explains that the Greek word translated "heaven" in English is often more literally "the heavens," as in "the kingdom of the heavens is at hand" (Willard's rendering of Matt. 4:17). Willard points out that in the original Greek of the New Testament, the kingdom "*of heaven* [singular]" is *tous ouranos,* which literally means kingdom "of the heavens [plural]."[2] This reflects the ancient view that the heavens were layered, much as we understand the various layers above us in the atmosphere: troposphere, stratosphere, mesosphere, and so on. Sphere, of course, is very similar to the word *realm.* The ancients imagined the invisible God inhabiting

PRAYER IS A WAY OF CONNECTING WITH GOD, WHO IS PRESENT HERE AND IN THE REALMS JESUS REFERRED TO AS HEAVENLY.

---

2. See Dallas Willard's discussion of heaven as "the heavens" in *The Divine Conspiracy: Rediscovering Our Hidden Life in God* (New York: HarperOne, 1998), 61–74.

the highest of these realms, understood to be just beyond the reach of the naked eye—just beyond what was conceived of as a dome in which the stars were thought to be permanently affixed, like those reflective stars on a child's ceiling that glow in the dark.

We see this view reflected in the writings of Paul, the author of several New Testament letters. Paul spoke of a mystical experience in prayer in which he understood himself to be in the third heaven. He adds mysteriously, "Whether it was in the body or out of the body I do not know" (2 Cor. 12:2 TNIV).

While God was understood to dwell in the highest of these heavenly realms and was thereby known as the Most High God, it was also understood that he could exist or cause his presence to be known all the way to the ground—to the lowest of the heavenly realms. Willard refers to this as "the air-filled space around us," including what fills our lungs when we breathe. (It's no accident that the Hebrew word for "spirit" also means "breath," as it does in the Greek language of the New Testament.)

Now we're getting somewhere. In the culture from which the Hebrew Scriptures emerged, it wasn't unusual to think that God would appear in various guises—usually shrouded in mystery but in some sense visible. For example, the patriarch Jacob met "a man" at the brook of Jabbok, and they wrestled all night (Gen. 32:22–24). There's ambiguity about this mystery man. Is he a man, an angel, or God? This same ambiguity is popping up in popular culture lately. Songs with words like "What if God were one of us, just a stranger on a bus?" Or in the television series *Joan of Arcadia*, where God appeared one week as a janitor, the next as a bag lady.

Before we start making fun of the ancients for having such primitive worldviews, we should remember that worldviews are simply a set of lenses that help us make sense of a reality that is far beyond our limited capacity to take in. Our sensory apparatus has a very limited capacity to perceive reality. We can only take in a small slice of all the data streaming our way. It's the same with our worldviews. At best, they are approximations of reality. In a sense, our worldviews simply inform our imagination, which in turn affects our perceptions.

OUR WORLDVIEWS SIMPLY INFORM OUR IMAGINATION, WHICH IN TURN AFFECTS OUR PERCEPTIONS.

But here's the interesting part: science is informing us that there may be many dimensions beyond the space-time four (length, width, height, and time) hidden within and among these. These dimensions are invisible to the naked eye or any current instrumentation. String theory, a complicated theory about the micro-mini aspect of reality, suggests that at this level, there may be multiple dimensions beyond or within the space-time four. *Come on!* we nonscientists think. And they just say, "No, really!"

Another theory, called brane theory, suggests that our four-dimensional universe may be imbedded in a "membrane" that separates two other spaces of multiple dimensions.[3] This is no joke. It is a serious attempt by physicists to understand why gravity is inexplicably weak compared to the other forces. (I did learn about this late at night on cable, but it was the respected *Charlie Rose* show and not some sparkly eyed lecturer talking to an adoring but paid studio audience.)

---

3. For more on brane theory, see Michelle Thaler, "Gravity: Strength in Weakness," *Christian Science Monitor*, September 24, 2003. http://www.csmonitor.com/2003/0924/p25s01 stss.html (accessed on October 23, 2007).

The scientists are not looking for an explanation of spiritual phenomena; nor are they seeking to locate "heaven" in the sense of a realm in which God dwells. They get understandably nervous when their findings get dragged into conversations about spirituality. But I am not making the point that "heaven" has been discovered or that the realms the scientists are positing are the transcendent realms of the ancient biblical worldview. It's quite possible that such realms, if they in fact exist, will defy discovery through the scientific method for as long as science is practiced.

THE PHYSICAL UNIVERSE IS A WILDER AND WIDER PLACE THAN ONCE THOUGHT.

I'm simply making the point that our worldview—our way of conceiving of or imagining reality—is in the process of shifting in some dramatic ways. The physical universe is a wilder and wider place than once thought. Our way of imagining the universe is now more open to realities like those that provide the backdrop to the world as perceived by Jesus.

How does all this translate into how people today are able to experience God?

SHIFTING WORLDVIEWS AFFECT OUR EXPERIENCE OF GOD

The young man who leads our Friday night visits with homeless friends in Ann Arbor taught me a lot about how worldviews shape perceptions and experiences. Eric's father is an atheist. Eric's own atheism was therefore learned and not some passionate reaction against the excesses of religion. He grew up with little interest in or exposure to religion, all of which makes his experience especially instructive.

Eric was a "Deadhead," having attended more than fifty Grateful Dead concerts. Not to stereotype, but Eric during this time smoked a lot of marijuana. He describes living for years in a cloud of the stuff. He stopped smoking marijuana for about a week and during that week became curious about God; he even asked out loud, "God, are you there?" No response. Shortly thereafter, he returned to the marijuana cloud. A few years later, he realized he wouldn't make much headway getting a new job until he cleared his system again for the inevitable drug test.

After this background, Eric told me of a vivid spiritual experience. "Around that time," he said, "I started getting curious about God again. Then one day, I heard a voice say, *I'm here.*"

Eric instantly understood this as the answer to the question he asked years earlier: "God, are you there?"

When Eric recounted hearing *I'm here*, he pointed, ever so slightly with his finger, away from his body. He then described how those two words changed his life. He felt that the main message of Christianity, Jesus, was true. He decided to start living as though that were the case. He swore off marijuana and has been drug-free ever since (a matter of years now). His life took on a much clearer focus and sense of purpose. He essentially hopped right onto the path of Jesus brand spirituality.

I asked him, "When you say, 'God said, *I'm here*,' what was the hearing experience like? An inner voice?"

"Yes," Eric replied, though his eyes said otherwise. So I pressed him.

"All right," he said. "I say it was an inner voice, so people don't think I'm crazy. Actually it felt like it came from right next to me."

Bingo. Eric grew up with a worldview that in some important respects is closer to the ancient worldview than the one in the process of receding or undergoing a major adjustment. Before these recent shifts took place, the modern worldview said, "What you see is what you get. Everything material is predictable, and with enough information we'll be able to squeeze all the mystery out of it. There is no God in heaven, because we've been up there, and no God was sighted."

But Eric grew up watching *Star Trek*, the television series that introduced popular culture to the new physics that began with Einstein. He knew all about space-time bending, multiple dimensions, wormholes, and quantum uncertainty from *Star Trek*. So when Eric heard, *I'm here,* as though from a space right next to him, he had the worldview to allow such a perception to land and take hold.

And take hold it did. You should have seen Eric in action the other Friday night leading the homeless ministry. He was their pastor. He was a breath of fresh God-air to those homeless people who love him because he so obviously loves them. One of the homeless men claims Eric prayed for his injured eye and his eye got better right away; the man reported that he stopped pickling himself in alcohol since then without even intending to. (No one is claiming any instant healing, just the possibility of a touch from God through Eric.)

When Jesus prayed, he went somewhere. That is, he got in touch with God who dwells in the heavenly realms, from the highest, most transcendent heavens down to the air-filled space around him. We can think of prayer as something we do that helps us become aware of being at the intersection of the world as we know it when we're sorting through the mail, and the world as we know it when God is passing through.

WHERE DID JESUS GO WHEN HE "ASCENDED"?

One of the things that embarrassed even devout Christians in the pre–*Star Trek* era was the ascension of Jesus. As the New Testament tells us, Jesus was crucified, died, and on the third day rose again from the dead. Then he ascended into heaven where he sits at the right hand of the Father.[4]

The original source material says, "After he said this, he was taken up before their very eyes, and a cloud hid him from their sight" (Acts 1:9).

According to this source, some phenomenon occurred whereby the risen but visible Jesus slipped out of view before the disciples' eyes. "Taken up" doesn't necessarily mean "took off like a rocket into outer space." They may have perceived a shift, which their worldview helped them interpret as "up." As this occurred, the atmosphere around him (or them) became cloudy and he slipped out of view.[5] If we were translating this phenomenon into Eric's worldview, we might add, "into another dimension." A dimension alongside yet transcending our space-time four.

---

4. This language is from the Apostle's Creed, a very ancient summary of the earliest faith of the Jesus movement.

5. Often when the ancient writers spoke of the transcendent God drawing near, the intersection between the heavenly and earthly dimensions appeared as a cloud. It's interesting that cloud is the same metaphor that scientists use to describe the indescribable nature of the smallest "particles," which don't really act like particles at all.

We would be wise to hold on to all this loosely, because even the best worldview is just an approximation of reality. The phrase "one step closer to knowing" applies to worldviews as well as to pilgrims.

WHAT IF PRAYER IS A WAY OF GOING SOMEWHERE?

It is certainly the case that those first-generation followers of Jesus felt they were to follow him even after he disappeared from their sight. It is certainly the case that they understood him to be near still. They were still near to him, and he was still near to the Father. And this nearness was reflected in their understanding and experience of prayer.

What if prayer is something we do to station ourselves at the intersection between the world as we know it when we're sorting the mail and whatever dimension Jesus slipped into when he "ascended"?

What if prayer is a way of going somewhere? Not the ordinary way of going somewhere by walking or driving a car, but more like going online. Going through a portal, in this case Jesus, on to a network of connections that has its origins in God as revealed by Jesus (Father, Son, Holy Spirit), and extending outward to any who want to be included in this expanding community.

THE BREADTH DIMENSION OF PRAYER

To explore prayer in a way that can be understood—even experienced—as "going somewhere," you can introduce prayer practices that were developed within a worldview that made sense of such a thing. These tend to be the ancient prayer practices. The recent interest in these practices isn't accidental. It's not simply that we're tired of contemporary prayer and are now trying the older methods. Or that "ancient is the new future." It's that recent shifts in our worldview correspond to an earlier, premodern worldview in which God's nearness *made sense.*

RECENT SHIFTS IN OUR WORLDVIEW CORRESPOND TO AN EARLIER, PREMODERN WORLDVIEW IN WHICH GOD'S NEARNESS *MADE SENSE.*

To pray as Jesus and his earliest followers did, and many more down through the centuries, we can learn a lesson from the Muslims and pray at intervals through the day. (Muslims have kept at this ancient practice of prayer at intervals through the day better than most Christians.)

Start, in other words, with the breadth dimension.

As an observant Jew, Jesus would have prayed at intervals through the day. It's likely he paused at least three times, possibly more, to recite the Shema, the closest thing to the creed of Israel: "Hear, O Israel: The LORD our God, the LORD is one. Love the LORD your God with all your heart and and with all your soul and with all your strength" (Deut. 6:4–5). Jesus added an important line to the Shema: "Love your neighbor as yourself" (Matt. 22:39).

We know the first generation of Jesus' followers prayed at intervals through the day. Throughout the Roman Empire, including ancient Israel, the bells sounded at intervals through the day: at sunrise, 9:00 a.m., noon, 3:00 p.m., and sundown. These corresponded to the more or less fixed intervals of prayer practiced at the time.

We find the early followers gathered at nine in the morning for prayers on the day of Pentecost, when the heavens opened and the Spirit came down on them all and they felt *very* close to God (Acts 2).

We find two disciples going to the temple for the 3:00 p.m. prayers (Acts 3:1). They met a person in great need and healed him on the way.

We find Peter going to a rooftop in Joppa for the midday prayers (Acts 10:9). The heavens opened, and he had a vision in which he must have felt frightfully close to God, who instructed him to let the Gentiles—the non-Jewish outsiders, previously excluded—into the messianic community forming around Jesus.

The book of Acts recounting these prayer experiences is something like the highlight film that includes the most interesting and dramatic things that happened when they prayed at intervals through the day. We can only hope for their sakes it wasn't like that all the time. No one could keep up with it.

I find it very interesting that Alcoholics Anonymous also practices a form of prayer at intervals through the day. The prayer traditions of AA include a time to pray in the morning before the day begins (using suggested set prayers) and praying at the end of the day before retiring (to review the events of the day in prayer). Prayers such as the "Serenity Prayer" are recommended for use through the day, a practice called "checking in with God."

Alcoholics Anonymous is a form of spirituality that has been stripped of as much of the traditional garb of religion as is possible, The purpose of this stripping process is to make spirituality accessible to alcoholics who typically either use religion as something to hide behind or fear it because they can't measure up to its demands. After all the stripping-down process, if something remains as part of an alcoholic's recovery, one has the sense that it's pretty important. Prayer at intervals through the day is one of those things.

I'm no expert on this kind of praying, having just begun practicing it in the year 2000, shortly after my father passed away. I found myself in a mild depression, lacking energy to pray. This is not a good thing, especially if you are being paid to be a Christian as I am, being a pastor.[6] I kept this practice to myself for a while. I considered it cheating. I was part of a spiritual tradition that valued spontaneous prayer in one's own words. I practice this still, perhaps even more than I used to, but I've added set prayers at intervals throughout the day to my prayer repertoire; I am reusing prayers prayed by others, such as the Psalms and the Lord's Prayer.

There are many prayer books that facilitate this practice. My favorite is *The Divine Hours*, compiled by Phyllis Tickle.[7] I discovered things I never anticipated through this practice. I was able to relax with this kind of prayer. It didn't depend as much on my state of mind or my feelings of spirituality at the time of prayer. It felt like dipping my canoe into a river of prayer that has been flowing since the time of Abraham.

It didn't depend on my own words, because I wasn't using them. I was using the words of others. I found that over time you can't pray using the words of others without becoming aware of the others whose words you are using.

---

6. I like to believe that I would still want to be a pastor even if I weren't being paid. The people who are not being paid are my heroes.

7. Phyllis Tickle, comp., *The Divine Hours* (Shippensburg, PA: Image, 2006). Much of what I've learned about prayer I've learned from Phyllis Tickle. You notice I keep referencing her.

It's like being a U2 fan. You listen to their songs, learn the lyrics, and sure enough you begin to feel like you know these guys. Bono is your friend. It doesn't seem fair: you know him so well that you feel he ought to at least recognize you, maybe call you up and try out a new set of lyrics on you.

Connections form through words. Words spoken by one person enter the inner world of another, and a bond between persons is forged. So you are not just praying alone (you, conversing with God in your head). You are praying with the words of others and increasingly with an awareness of the company of others. A text in the New Testament letter to the Hebrews, reflecting this experience, says, "Since we are surrounded by such a great cloud of witnesses, let us throw off everything that hinders" (Heb. 12:1). Some kind of uplift comes to us through an awareness of others.

As this practice of prayer through the day becomes part of your daily rhythm, there is a natural and growing awareness that these words are shared with others around the world who also use them; this cascade of prayer goes through space as well as time. The power of these prayers is not limited to their original inspiration but includes their use by many down the years and across the planet through others to whom we are connected in love. They are living words.

I'm sure this must be part of the power of prayer in the fellowship of Alcoholics Anonymous. Alcoholism is a very isolating disease/disorder. When alcoholics seeking recovery pray in the morning or the evening using the prayers of others engaged in the same battle, they do so with a growing awareness that they are not alone. Others are struggling with them, and they are strengthened.

Prayer may thus become an experience of stepping into a network of connections between persons. The network includes those who were first inspired to pray with these words, those who have "gone before" but remain in God's care, and those who make them their own today. One even imagines that those who are loved by anyone thus connected are in some fashion included in the community of prayer. Ruling over all and working through all is the original source of personal connections: God.

This reality may or may not be experienced at any given time of prayer. It may have varying levels of intensity. But the possibility that it may be experienced at any given time of prayer, included in one's worldview, makes the phenomenon that much more likely. The dim or wispy instances of this phenomenon, once relegated to the periphery of our worldview, are given a more prominent place as our worldview shifts. This enhances our experience of the phenomenon.

PRAYER MAY THUS BECOME AN EXPERIENCE OF STEPPING INTO A NETWORK OF CONNECTIONS BETWEEN PERSONS.

All of this is wrapped up in "saying your prayers." Begin once a day, whenever it is easiest. Leverage your current habits first, either that morning cup of coffee or the fact that you go to bed every night. Add a second time and, once that's part of your routine, a third. I observe four to five intervals of prayer through the day, but that's only after years of making space in my day. This kind of prayer is like regular eating—driven by neediness, not holiness. Each interval can be a mere "touch point"; any one set of prayers can be said in the time it takes to boil water for tea (longer is also permissible). Pray as you can, not as you can't.

DEPTH DIMENSION

Once the breadth dimension of prayer has gained a foothold, be alert to the inclination to go deeper. Having a taste of connection, however fleeting, whets your appetite for more. Take the awareness of an appetite for more as an invitation from God to go deeper.

This began to happen with me several years ago, mainly in the morning. For years I had aimed at setting aside time in the morning for devotions. I did it because I wanted to and because I knew it was good for me. It was easy to skip, and I did often, but I kept returning to this practice. But the invitation to go deeper, experienced only fleetingly or sporadically in the past, became a daily occurrence. I found myself getting up earlier and earlier in anticipation of this time. (It probably didn't hurt that as I got older, I *couldn't* sleep in. All things work together for good.) A shift was happening in my experience of prayer. I wasn't just doing something good for me. I was going somewhere.

The first depth probe is the spiritual discipline of stillness. This is reflected in the line from the psalm: "Be still, and know that I am God" (Ps. 46:10). The French philosopher-mathematician Blaise Pascal said, "I have discovered that all the unhappiness of men arises from one single fact, that they are unable to stay quietly in their own room."

When you turn off the television and the cell phone and the e-mail and try to sit quietly in your own room, you notice your mind running wild like a toddler whose mother is trying to talk on the phone, taking every advantage. Physical stillness is one thing (and the place to start), but how do you still your mind?

The Eastern Orthodox tradition (part of the liturgical quadrant) recommends the use of the Jesus Prayer for this purpose. The Jesus Prayer is a simple one-line prayer: "Lord Jesus Christ, Son of God, have mercy on me a sinner." This prayer can be said meditatively, linking the words of the prayer to one's breathing. Inhale: *Lord Jesus Christ, Son of God*; exhale: *have mercy on me a sinner*. You can do this for as long as you like. Try it—you might like it.

The point of the prayer is to focus attention away from your thoughts and toward God, who has an existence apart from your thoughts. It's a way of slowing the pace of your thoughts so they demand less of your attention. This practice can be thought of as inner stillness.

In my experience, thoughts don't necessarily stop, but they do slow down, and the attention they demand decreases. Time can pass without much awareness of its passing. Breathing and heart rate slow. A calm settles over you, and in the calm a sense of connection happens. This is the experience of inner stillness, and as the psalm suggests, it gives space for God to be known.

The Eastern Orthodox speak of prayer as a "descent with the mind into the heart." This language is strange to our ears because it reflects a premodern worldview that understands prayer as activity by which we go somewhere. The inner world was understood to be a more mysterious and glorious place and a portal through which to connect with heavenly things.

"Descent with the mind into the heart" is a vivid description of what can happen in a time of inner stillness: a movement perceived as a gentle descent from a state of consciousness in which busy thoughts demand attention, to an experience of greater inward calm, perceived as more centrally located in the body. The mind has not been "turned off," but thoughts have slowed; these accompany you to a different realm of experience.[8] This realm is a place where God can more easily get a word, or an image, or a wordless impression in edgewise.

The body, after all, is *somewhere*. "Inner world" language isn't just metaphor. The body is a place in which awareness happens. Personal connections happen here. The temple in ancient Israel was a physical place where God was understood to dwell especially. The body is a temple—a place within which God may dwell. Is it so odd to think that there would be *experience* corresponding to this reality?

> THE BODY IS A TEMPLE, A PLACE WITHIN WHICH GOD MAY DWELL. IS IT SO ODD TO THINK THAT THERE WOULD BE *EXPERIENCE* CORRESPONDING TO THIS REALITY?

Another way to go deeper in prayer involves meditating on a short text of Scripture. This practice is called *lectio divina*, Latin for "divine reading"—a sacred form of reading that is prayerful. It's more like tasting a fine wine than combing a text for information. It is a savoring, meditative process rather than an analytical one, where words are experienced as much as they are thought.

Pick a biblical text that your heart is already drawn to. Often one with vivid visual imagery, like Psalm 23, works well. Read the text slowly a few times, paying attention to any affective or feeling

---

8. Wisely, the Eastern Orthodox caution against any attempt to "turn off the mind"; it is understood that during prayer of this kind, the mind is to remain watchful; spiritual experience is not universally good, and the mind is required to discern.

responses to the words—even the slightest or most subtle sense of being drawn to a particular portion. Then read that smaller portion over slowly. In Psalm 23, it might be the opening verses: "The LORD is my shepherd, I lack nothing. He makes me lie down in green pastures, he leads me beside quiet waters." Rather than try to understand what that means, place yourself through the use of your imagination within the scene. See yourself being led to lie down in a green pasture next to a freshwater stream. Don't focus on getting something out of the experience. Focus on simply being there. Wonderful connections can happen in a time spent like this.

MYSTICISM IS MAKING A COMEBACK

Mystical experience is shot through the Hebrew Scriptures (the portion of the Bible that shaped Jesus) as well as the writings left in his wake. Jesus had mystical experiences. So did the apostles Peter and Paul and the others.

The movement spawned by Jesus seems to have multiplied mystical experience. This was understood as a fulfillment of a promise by God to "pour out my Spirit on all people" (Joel 2:28; Acts 2:17). After the rise of the enlightenment and rationalism, mysticism went underground. Wild-eyed mystics were relegated to monasteries where they were kept out of sight or celebrated as uniquely gifted individuals. This was the result of a shifting worldview that made little room for the stuff of mysticism, which is mystery. The mystery of God. The mystery of life. The mystery of the world.

Slowly but inexorably, mysticism is making a comeback. It's always been a messy affair, having to do with those things that defy reduction or explanation or mastery. And the resurgence of mysticism after a long period of hibernation is bound to be, shall we say, interesting, as together we find our bearings on the wild side of life.

MYSTICISM IS PART OF THE HUMAN EXPERIENCE. WE'RE WIRED FOR IT.

Ready or not, though, it's coming. Because mysticism is part of the human experience. We're wired for it. It's part of every religious tradition, and it's part of traditions that would deny any religious orientation. Secular ecologists are drawn to their field of study by mystical experiences of nature out in the field. Musicians and other artists, fishermen, golfers, hunters, athletes, gardeners, moviegoers—all have experiences that light up the mystical portions of the brain.

TO WHAT END?

Jesus brand spirituality isn't validated by its capacity to mediate mystical experience. We can't resolve the "my religion is better than yours" debate by measuring the frequency, intensity, or quality of our mystical experiences.

Jesus brand spirituality has more to do with shaping the aim, the direction, the trajectory of mystical experience. It answers the question, "To what end, this?" The end, simply put by Jesus himself, is love: love of God and neighbor.

Within Jesus brand spirituality, mysticism surely has a place. Jesus brand spirituality mediates mystical experience—connections with God, others, and all living things. But the place of this experience is within a story: the love story of God in search of humanity.

JESUS BRAND SPIRITUALITY STUDY QUESTIONS: CONTEMPLATIVE DIMENSION

If you are discussing these questions in a group, you may want to refer to the Discussion Ground Rules for guidance. These can be found in the appendix.

1. The author describes several factors that make it difficult for modern people to understand, talk about, and perceive "spiritual experience" [see pp. 89–96]. How have these or other factors influenced you?

2. The author describes a variety of experiences that are not ordinarily thought of as "mystical" [see pp. 96–98]. Have you ever experienced or felt something like that? If so, what was it like?

3. The author discusses changes in the way people understand the nature of reality [see pp. 107–15]. Do you think people in our society are more open to spiritual experience than previous generations? What factors do you think account for this?

4. What do you think of Phyllis Tickle's analogy of the Internet [see p. 108] as a way to understand how prayer might involve an experience of "going somewhere" as well as doing something?

5. What do you think of the author's recommendation to begin with the "breadth dimension" of prayer, that is, learning to pray at short intervals through the day [see pp. 116–21]?

6. Have you ever experienced a time of stillness and/or solitude that made you wish for more? What was it like, and how did it affect you?

BIBLICAL DIMENSION

7

A STORY RUNS THROUGH IT

One of the reasons people are nervous about reading the Bible, let alone allowing the message of the Bible into their inner world to shape the whole of life, is the glibness with which Christians say things like, "If everyone just followed God's plan in the Bible, everything would be fine."

The thought of everyone doing any one thing makes me nervous. Mobs are formed by everyone doing one thing. Everyone doing any one thing doesn't leave much room for error. Whatever one thing they understand themselves to be doing really needs to be precisely the thing that ought to be done.

The Bible refers to its own words as "sharper than any two-edged sword, piercing even to the division of soul and spirit, and of joints and marrow" (Heb. 4:12 NKJV). Picture the entire human race picking up the sharpest conceivable scalpel and seeking to make the world a better place by using it with the best of intentions.

I don't know about you, but I would take cover.

I think Jesus would advise us to take cover too. Jesus warned against people using the scalpel to take a speck of sawdust out of their brother's eye (Luke 6:41–42). He was used to the disciples approaching him with the best of intentions, their vision obscured by an ophthalmic plank of their own, armed with a rusty set of tweezers to go after the speck of dust in his eye.

FUNDAMENTALLY, THE BIBLE IS THE LOVE STORY OF GOD IN SEARCH OF HUMANITY.

Let us all blink a few times and then relax.

Anything understood to be inspired by God should be understood as very powerful. Anything that is very powerful should be handled with caution.

What is the Bible *fundamentally?* Not what does the Bible include or contain, but what *is* it? Is it a book we can pick up and use as though it were a patently obvious instruction manual for life? *The Bible: How to Be and What to Do in Every Situation.* Is the Bible God's plan for humanity in the way that an engineering blueprint is a plan for the construction of a building?

No. The Bible includes plans and instructions, but it is not fundamentally that.

I'm trying to be careful here, because this next part is important. I hope I'm not wrong. I may be, so please discern for yourself whether or not this make sense.

Fundamentally, the Bible is the love story of God in search of humanity. The Bible is not God's *plan* so much as it is God's *plot.*

A plan is a limited way to guide us as we encounter the incredible complexities of life. A plan is a static thing. In the military, a battle plan must often be thrown out once the battle is actually engaged.

A plot, however, is part of something living, adaptable, and richly textured: a story. A plot is the unfolding of a story. It can speak to a wide variety of people in a wide variety of circumstances. It can speak across the ages. The good plots are subtle, complex, offering many different points of contact for the listener. Stories don't just entertain us, though the good ones do that as well. They reveal connections we might otherwise not have noticed. They guide and shape us in ways that go much deeper than mere commands.

We are moved by stories more powerfully than we are moved by instructions. We sit in the movie theater, and as the story unfolds (if it's a good one) we're drawn in; we laugh and get choked up and feel connected with the characters; sometimes we even feel connected to our fellow moviegoers. The really great stories are open-ended. We finish the book or walk out of the movie theater into the blinding sun, determined to pick up where they left off.

We remember stories better than we remember instructions. We engage stories. We participate in them. We are story-driven, story-generating, story-craving, story-telling units. Stories, better than anything else, fit us.

Stories are what our brains use to help us come to grips with reality. Whether the story is in the form of fable, historical narrative, or what happened at work today, stories as a whole are about the same thing: making sense of the world. Stories are about the connection between things. Without them, life seems like a series of disconnected events. In our bones, and in our stories, we know otherwise.

The Bible is not the only story in town. But by any measure, the love story of God in search of humanity is a leading candidate for the title *The Greatest Story Ever Told.* It can be thought of as a story that connects all the others. To suggest there is no such thing as an all-encompassing story is a hallmark of contemporary thought, but it goes against the grain of the human brain, which is constantly seeking out connections. While, some may claim that there is no such thing as any one story that connects all the others, the brain is inevitably in the process of searching out such a story.

JESUS BRAND SPIRITUALITY IS CENTERED ON THE PERSON OF JESUS, WHO TRANSFORMS THE BIBLE AND BECOMES THE LENS THROUGH WHICH WE READ IT.

The Bible tells a story of a work in progress. It's in the very nature of stories to unfold. Sometimes a turn of events takes place within a story that transforms it. What began as tragedy can turn into comedy and vice versa. A compelling twist in a plot casts a different light on all that went before. That's part of the thrill of stories: they take us somewhere; the scenery changes; the plot thickens.

Jesus is such a twist in the plot of the love story of God in search of humanity. Jesus doesn't just appear in the story; he transforms the story.

Jesus brand spirituality isn't centered on the Bible, per se. Jesus brand spirituality is centered on the person of Jesus, who transforms the Bible and becomes the lens through which we read it.

The illustration of religion as a rope of three cords held together by a story is apt because it gives story its proper place. It's what holds everything together.

When people of faith treat the Bible as lawyers treat the venerable tradition of case law[1]—as something to master, as the fodder with which to advance an argument—I want to pull my hair out. It is the love story of God in search of humanity.

THE STORY OF GOD IN SEARCH OF HUMANITY IN FIVE ACTS[2]

Act 1: The Primordial Garden

Once upon a time, Lord Adam, Lady Eve, and Lord Yahweh, also known as the Lord Most High, were together in a garden. "There's a place for us, somewhere a place for us," the garden sang.

When young children take a few dining room chairs to the living room and make a tent over the chairs with a blanket, when they beg their parents to let them play in the empty box that came with the new refrigerator, they are responding to this song. *There's a place for us, somewhere a place for us.* There's a place like that garden where all is well and we can walk in peace and harmony with God, with others, with all living things, and therefore, with ourselves.

The once-upon-a-time garden had a river running through it, and from this river abundant life flowed into all the world.

But something went horribly wrong in the garden. This place, held together by love, which requires trust, was violated. The earliest

---

1. Some of my best friends are lawyers. Lawyers are much maligned of late, but are never more loved than when you need one.

2. I am grateful to N. T. Wright for his rendering of the message of the Bible in five acts, detailed in *The Last Word: Beyond the Bible Wars to a New Understanding of the Authority of Scripture* (New York: HarperOne, 2005), 121–26. Wright's telling is quite a bit different than my telling; his five acts include: (1) creation, (2) fall, (3) Israel, (4) Jesus, and (5) the church. With a story so full of meaning, there are innumerable ways to do the telling.

homo sapiens ("man, the wise") did an unwise thing. They took the one thing that had been forbidden them, fruit from the tree of the knowledge of good and evil. God's first words to them had been, "You may freely eat of anything, except . . ."

They took fruit from the forbidden tree of knowledge. They took knowledge they weren't ready for, the first breach of trust. That's the sad part of the wonderful story of knowledge down to this day. We have a tendency to grasp for knowledge, technology, new ways of thinking and doing that we just don't seem to be ready for. Things meant for good have a tendency to spoil in our hands like fruit on the window sill.

One of our great prophets saw a river running through the garden and called it justice: "Let justice roll on like a river, righteousness like a never-failing stream!" (Amos 5:24). Our ancestors polluted the river running through the garden with the first breach of trust, the first violation of love, the first act of injustice.

The human-divine relationship was polluted with fear as the humans hid from God in the garden for the first time. Their relationship with each other was polluted by blame as they wagged their fingers at each other. Their relationship with self was polluted as they felt personal shame for the first time.

And something happened to humanity's relationship with other living things. This is shrouded in mystery, but as the story is told, the Lord Yahweh, seeing their feeble attempts to hide behind a few fig leaves, gave them instead the pelt of an animal for clothing. And the echo of an innocent losing its life resounded through the garden.

End of act 1, the man and the woman, exiled beyond the eastern gate of the garden, the way back in closed for now. (Time being God's way of saying there's no way back, only forward.) We imagine Lord Yahweh, perhaps outside the western wall of the garden, feeling his own sense of loss, his own form of homelessness on earth. We imagine God missing them, his humans.

Act 2: Ezekiel's Visionary Garden-Temple

Years passed, back in the era when no one was counting. Centuries. Millennia.

Wherever the humans went, they brought their festering wound with them. The breach of trust. The alienation. The longing for home even when they had one.

Yet another crisis ensued. The seed of the woman had become a nation, Israel, representing all the people on the earth. Their temple in Jerusalem was surrounded by the Babylonian hosts, injustice having proliferated. The people of Israel were on the verge of yet another exile.

Outside the camp, far away in Babylon, on the eve of the temple's destruction, one of the children of Israel, a priest and a prophet named Ezekiel, had a vision. In the vision he was called by God "son of man," or one who represents all of humanity (Ezek. 2:1, 3, 6, 8).

In this vision, God showed this son of man a temple that was larger than life itself. A temple that seemed as much a garden as anything else because it had no roof. In its walls were towering gates that no one could miss. As if God were saying, *There's a way back into this place. Let me show you.*

Because it was a temple as well as a garden, there was an altar. As altars often are, this one was shrouded in an awful mystery. It was an altar where innocents lost their lives to cover the shame of the guilty. A life for a life. As if justice demands a price be paid for injustice to be undone.

Like that other place, the garden place, there was a river running through it, with headwaters surging from the base of the altar. A river even more prominent than the river running through the original garden. A river that got deeper and deeper the farther out it flowed, drawing attention to the great deep beyond the garden-temple walls.

It was as if God were saying through the son of man's vision: *Don't forget the dream of a place for us, somewhere a place for us. Lift up your heads, strengthen your drooping knees, keep your eyes open. Something's coming, something good.*

Act 3: Jesus in Herod's Temple

Now time had passed that may be counted in hundreds of years. Jesus of Nazareth, another son of man, had been teaching in the temple courts. This was Israel's rebuilt temple. The people of Israel had mixed feelings about this temple, because it was the project of King Herod, a trumped-up puppet of the Roman overlords, a mere figurehead king who served at the pleasure of the occupation force. Though they were back in their homeland, the people of Israel were still in a kind of exile. They had yet to find what they were looking for—the garden place of their dreams.

It was, fittingly, the Feast of Tabernacles, high holy days, when the people of Israel streamed in to their temple in Jerusalem, carrying with them sheaves to serve as little booths, little tabernacles for the pilgrimage to the big one.

It was, we're told, the last and great day of the feast—the day when the priests of Israel made festal procession from the temple courts to a pool outside the gates from which they returned with pitchers full of water. To the sound of trumpets and singing, to the joy of the dance they returned, up to the horns of the altar to pour out their water at the altar's base. It is as though they were reminding themselves of the river running through the visionary garden-temple, which in turn reminded them of the river running through the primordial garden. It is as though God wanted to keep this hope alive: *there's a place for us, somewhere a place for us.*

On this day, the last and great day of the feast, perhaps at this moment when the people looked longingly at the little stream of water trickling from the base of the altar in their temple, it is recorded that Jesus stood up and with a loud voice cried, "If anyone is thirsty, let him come to me and drink. Whoever believes in me, as the Scripture has said, streams of living water will flow from within him" (John 7:37–38 NIV).

As if to say, *There's a place for us—and the way is open to any who would come. A garden is planted in our hearts, and a river is running through it . . .*

Act 4: The Easter Garden

Time was speeding up now, measured in weeks or days. The Son of man had offered himself, an innocent life for the sins of the world, the whole gasping and dying, sad and suffering, world-weary world. The longstanding wound in the pain-filled heart of God was visible now, an awful stream of mercy in the form of blood and pleural fluid pouring from the lanced side of Jesus.

Less than two full days had passed, spanning three. It was early, the first day of a new week. A woman, Mary Magdalene, had gone to a garden, where Jesus, a man she loved, was buried. It was early and still dark. The woman was weeping a river of tears.

Through her tears, she saw the stone barring entrance to the tomb out of place. She peered into the tomb to find it empty. Terrified, she ran to the others, the men. Peter and John returned to the garden with her and peered into the empty tomb and saw burial cloths oddly arranged, undisturbed. The napkin meant for the head was neatly folded in its place.

Confused, they returned to the safety of the others. But Mary remained, now weeping uncontrollably, inconsolably.

Two men in white appeared. Angels?

"Why so sad?" they asked.

"They've taken away my Lord, and I cannot find him!" Mary replied.

At this, she turned around and saw someone in her peripheral vision, or perhaps just beyond it . . .

"Woman, who are you looking for?"

Thinking it was the gardener—the gardener!—she said, "Sir, if you've taken him somewhere, tell me that I may get him."

"Mary," he said.

And with that one word, her heart melted, and we can only imagine that her tears ran down like a torrent.

"Rabboni!" (which means, Teacher) she answered, fulfilling the cry of her people when they sang, "Those who sow with tears/ will reap with songs of joy./ Those who go out weeping,/ carrying seed to sow,/ will return with songs of joy,/ carrying sheaves with them" (Ps. 126:5–6).

There's a place for us, and a river runs through it. And all shall be well.

Interlude

And now let me intrude on this story with a story of my own about a man who cried a river of tears.

It was the year 2000. My brother-in-law Bill, who is on the cynical side—charmingly so, endearingly so—had been shaken to the core. His son Nate, brought up believing nothing in particular about God, said in his senior year of high school, "Dad, I feel like there's something missing, and that something may be God. Would you read this book that's been making sense to me?" It was a book about God.

Bill read the book, and it made sense to him. Of course he didn't tell me that. He was playing it close to the vest, knowing I'm in the God business and might be overeager to hear his God-talk. On more than one occasion he has ribbed me about my God preoccupation.

But he had to move to another state for his job, a full year before his family could join him. He asked me to recommend a church.

I was floored to hear Bill talking like this. I suggested a church I was familiar with. He went and didn't like it.

I told him, "Look for another church, then." He said he'd look for one.

I was dying to know what was going on with this guy, but he was keeping his own counsel.

One night on the phone, he asked me, "Ken, how do you manage all the hard things you hear from people in distress all the time? How do you handle that emotionally?"

I told him it used to be harder before God uncorked something some years back and I started crying. Then I talked for about ten solid minutes about my intimate God experiences involving crying. Once, I told him, for six months straight, I cried for about an hour and a half like clockwork every Wednesday when I prayed. I cried so long and hard my worried wife knocked on the door of my office: "Ken, are you all right?"

"Yes, I'm fine. It's all good," I'd say. And it was, but I couldn't tell you why.

As I was talking like this, recounting my own intimate God experiences crying, I was thinking, *Why am I talking like this to Bill? Surely talk like this will frighten him off any God path! Surely this storytelling will come back to haunt me!* But I kept on blabbing about blubbering. And then I fell silent.

Bill didn't say anything. We then played phone chicken. Who would give in and break the awkward silence first? Not me. I had said too much already. I'd just as soon not say anything else to Bill for the rest of my life.

Finally, Bill said, "Funny you should mention it, Ken. Because this past Sunday I cried for the first time in forty years."

With patience on my part and questioning, Bill went on to tell his story. He told of attending a particular church and how he enjoyed singing the songs. At times, it was like a cat was rubbing up the back of his legs causing a little shiver when he sang those songs. Finally, he told of how he went up to the altar rail when the priest asked for anyone to come who wished to receive a prayer of blessing. And how, once there, Bill decided he wanted to step into the story of God in search of humanity and allow himself to be found. And a great release of waterworks commenced at that altar.

To what end? you may ask, and wisely. Was this but the first of many religious experiences, like so many religious experiences that seem to get people addicted to religious experience such that they make the pursuit of such experiences a kind of life quest, until eventually they run out of experiences or the appetite for them?

Thankfully, no, not in Bill's case.

Because I forgot to mention that Bill, though he works as a

high-powered businessman in the technology sector, received his doctorate in fine arts. In poetry, thank you. As a man of letters, Bill understands a story when he sees one.[4] He understands the power of a story to shape our lives.

Bill understood that he had accepted an invitation to step into the love story of God in search of humanity. He understood that his tears were like Mary's tears in the garden. They were part of the river running through the garden: a river of trust restored, and love, and justice renewed on the earth.

So Bill got going. He volunteered to help Mini, who went to a drug-infested neighborhood every Saturday and set up shop to run a program for young children who needed attention. Week after week, as long as he was in that town, Bill helped Mini help the children know they were loved.

Then Bill's job took him to Cedar Rapids, Iowa. There, Bill volunteered in hospice, sitting with dying patients in their homes or hospital rooms to provide a little relief to their distraught family members. Bill noticed that there wasn't a hospice facility in his new hometown, so he made some phone calls, and before you knew it, he was circulating a petition of support to build a hospice facility, and then he was on a committee to raise funds to build one. And it came to pass.

In his work in intellectual property for a high-tech firm, Bill noticed that there were a few new technologies that, when connected, might have the capacity to help manage traffic in congested cities so as to reduce carbon emissions. At the time of this writing, he's working to see that happen.

---

4. Bill has posted some of his poetic prose at http://mysticalshmystical.blogspot.com/.

Bill understands that by stepping into the love story of God in search of humanity, he's being empowered to lend a hand to Jesus, who is all about repairing the world. Bill understands that it's a drama in five acts, four of which have already occurred, with the fifth act on the way. And he's helping to write the story because he's been pulled into it—not to observe it, but to participate in its unfolding.

Act 5: The Garden City to Come
Now we cut to the indeterminate future, whether measured in years or decades or millennia or perhaps in some other frame than time; we won't know until it happens. A surprise is to be expected.

Close your eyes and envision a city come down from the realms beyond. A heavenly Jerusalem, if you will, come to earth. A garden city with a river running through it, and trees that are for the healing of the nations lining the banks of the river (Rev. 22:2). Imagine the righting of great wrongs, to scale. The end of war, oppression, and violence, of all things false and ugly.

Imagine, if you will, the reintegration of heaven and earth. Not a return to things past, because time, so far as we know, always keeps us moving forward. Imagine a future where all is finally well with God, with others, and with all living things, and therefore with ourselves.

There. You know enough of the story to participate in its unfolding if you want to.

You may open your eyes now and lend a hand until you see it happen.

8

THE BOOK JESUS TRANSFORMED

I love the children's song, "Jesus loves me, this I know, for the Bible tells me so." Except that it doesn't work like that anymore.

The reasoning goes like this: *The Bible is the Word of God. The Bible teaches that Jesus loves us. Therefore Jesus loves me, this I know.*

That approach worked in the Christianized West for a long time. But it's no longer a worldview assumption for many—not in my hometown, at least.

Let's face it: the Bible in human hands has been badly misused. Back when Galileo challenged the view that the earth was the center of the solar system, he was rebuked by a leader of the church with these words: "To affirm that the earth revolves very swiftly around the sun is a dangerous thing, not only irritating the theologians and philosophers, but injuring our holy faith and making the sacred scripture false."[1] For a long time, the church lent tacit, even

---

1. Cardinal Bellarmine, in a letter to Galileo.

explicit approval to the institution of slavery on the grounds that Scripture supported its legitimacy. For an even longer time, women were viewed as inferior to men based on a widely accepted reading of Scripture.

Before we pile on and declare the Bible hopelessly vulnerable to corruption, we might remind ourselves that anything in human hands can be misused. We've done things in the name of love and beauty and freedom that only bring about hate and ugliness and more oppression.

RELIGION IS NO ESCAPE FROM THE MESSY BUSINESS OF HUMANITY.

Something as wonderful and powerful as science has been misused. Science created the technologies that now threaten our existence. Through science we hope to undo some of the damage that science made possible in much the same way that we've appealed to Scripture to overturn wrongs previously supported by our use of Scripture.

Religion is no escape from the messy business of humanity.

So how do we approach this powerful book, the Bible? Do we replace it with the latest trusted repository of wisdom? We certainly could, but this would completely undermine the spirituality that Jesus modeled. It was, after all, the book that shaped him.

Do we treat the Bible as a relic of the past to be revered as relics are venerated? This has the feel of reverence, but it's an empty honor. Why not simply renounce the Bible outright and move on? Or do we leave the Bible, like radioactive material, in the hands of experts?

THE BIBLE IN THE EXPERT HANDS OF JESUS

Perhaps we could leave the Bible in the expert hands of Jesus and let him read it to us or learn to discern the message of the Bible only in closest connection with him. Perhaps we could read the Bible as the book Jesus transformed.

When the Bible refers to Jesus as the Word made flesh, dwelling among us (John 1:14), it is speaking of a transformative event in our understanding of the Bible itself.

The literary critic C. S. Lewis saw the Christian story as the author of the play stepping onto the stage as one of the characters in the drama.[2] Jesus didn't simply adopt a part already written like the director Quentin Tarantino does in his movies. Jesus enters the play as the playwright, the director, and the protagonist. He is the storyteller, and he is the main character whose actions reshape the plot. He invites us into the drama, onto the stage, as players in a supporting role.

JESUS INVITES US TO SEE OUR LIVES IN . . . THE STORY IN WHICH HE PARTICIPATES, SO THAT WE TOO CAN BECOME PLAYERS IN THE STORY.

As the Word made flesh and dwelling among us, Jesus invites us to see our lives in a new light, to understand our significance within the story he tells, the story in which he participates, so that we too can become players in the story.

---

2. C. S. Lewis, *Mere Christianity* (New York: HarperOne, 2001), 65.

A development of this magnitude in the love story of God in search of humanity is truly transformative.

Transformation implies change, and all change involves some loss, and all loss involves some grief. Which is exactly what Jesus got from the guardians of biblical truth whenever he transformed the meaning of the book in their hands. The Pharisees, despite a lot of bad press, were the most popular Bible teachers in their day. Their reading of Scripture had much in common with Jesus'. As a young man, Jesus no doubt learned from the Pharisees. Perhaps because they were so close in their views of the Bible, the Pharisees seem to have felt the most threatened by his divergent views.

In one heated exchange with the Pharisees over the Bible, Jesus said, "You diligently study the Scriptures because you think that by them you possess eternal life. These are the Scriptures that testify about me, yet you refuse to come to me to have life" (John 5:39–40 NIV).

People who have committed themselves to the pursuit of God have to look out for some occupational hazards. One is the tendency to seek mastery. God, or the things of God, or the ways of God, can be viewed as the subject matter, and our task is to master the subject as though it were any other subject—say, thermal dynamics. When presented with something as tangible as a sacred text, it's difficult to restrain the impulse to seek mastery.

The Bible is not a book we can master like that. The Bible tells a story and invites us into it. As we step into the story, we encounter the storyteller. If there's any mastering to be done, it's not us of it, and even less, us of him.

The guardians of biblical truth viewed Jesus as someone who took liberties with the Bible. This is exactly what you would expect of the storyteller entering the story as the protagonist. He's not here to play the part as it's been understood and conceived by the audience to this point. He's here to shake things up, to bring *drama* to the drama, to resolve old tensions and add new ones, to bring the element of surprise.

Jesus didn't feel obliged to bow to the conventional wisdom of the Bible experts of his day. He read the Bible differently than his elders did. "You have heard that it was said, 'Love your neighbor and hate your enemy,'" said Jesus, quoting those quoting tradition. "But I tell you," said Jesus, "'love your enemies and pray for those who persecute you'" (Matt. 5:43–44). This kind of approach to the Bible was not intended to gain the favor of his elders. It was purposefully provocative language designed to highlight a plot twist in the story signaled by his arrival.

JESUS, LORD OF THE BIBLE

Jesus and his disciples were walking through a field one Sabbath day, picking a few heads of grain to satisfy their hunger. The Pharisees accused him of breaking the Sabbath. Jesus responded by making an extraordinary claim: that he, the Son of man, was Lord of the Sabbath, since the Sabbath was given to serve man and not man to serve the Sabbath (Mark 2:23–28).

Today, people of faith don't vigorously debate what it means to observe the Sabbath as they once did. Other issues seem to have our attention. Claims of lordship over the Sabbath don't threaten us as they would have threatened the Pharisees, because we don't see any hallowed Sabbath practices affected by this claim.

If Jesus is Lord, wouldn't it follow that he is Lord, in some tangible, transformative, and potentially upsetting way, of the Bible?

IF JESUS IS LORD, WOULDN'T IT FOLLOW THAT HE IS LORD, IN SOME TANGIBLE, TRANSFORMATIVE, AND POTENTIALLY UPSETTING WAY, OF THE BIBLE?

What would such a thing mean? It would mean that Jesus has the authority to read, interpret, and apply the message of the Bible. He asserted this authority in the face of the prevailing readings of the Bible in his time. There's no reason to think he wouldn't step in and overrule our readings of the Bible, including readings that we hold near and dear.

For example, we have settled on different systems or ways of approaching the Bible as the best safeguards to determine what God is in fact saying through the Bible. As Lord of the Bible, Jesus would be free to work through or within these systems, but he is surely not constrained by them.

THE TWO PRIMARY SAFEGUARD SYSTEMS

Christians, like everyone else throughout the centuries, have wrestled with the question of authority. Who is to say what God's will is? Two major solutions to this problem have been developed, one by Roman Catholicism, the other by Protantism.

Catholics have settled on the teaching authority of the properly authorized church leadership as the final authority. When the properly authorized church authority makes a pronouncement on a matter of biblical truth, under the properly delineated circumstances established by previous decisions, then we know we're on safe ground. Or so it goes.

Protestants have settled on the authority of the Bible itself as the final authority. But this begs the question: how do we determine what the Bible is teaching in a particular matter? To address this, a subsidiary safeguard is developed, an agreed-upon system of principles defining the nature of Scripture itself, in what sense it is inspired, and how it is to be read and interpreted. Follow the principles and we're on safe ground. Or so it goes.

In both cases, circular reasoning is at work. In the case of the first safeguard system, the church authorities are the ones who determine who the church authorities are. But which church authorities do the determining? Human conflict didn't end with the advent of the messianic movement. Jesus' disciples argued with each other in his presence. The earliest documents of the church bear witness to conflicts between leaders, including Peter and Paul. In the history of the church, two popes claiming mutually exclusive preeminence served simultaneously. The dispute was settled by a war. Hmm.

In the second safeguard system, the Bible itself teaches us how to interpret the Bible—except that it doesn't do so explicitly or exhaustively. We are left to infer what the principles might be. One of the primary New Testament writers uses an allegorical method of interpreting the Bible on at least one occasion that wouldn't be accepted in many seminaries today.[3]

It's important to learn from the biblical writers themselves how to best interpret the Bible, but shouldn't we also acknowledge that this

---

3. See Galatians 4:21–30 for an example of Paul's allegorical use of Scripture.

isn't the simple, straightforward, and obvious process we sometimes imply that it is?

I'm not trying to be difficult by bringing up the challenging questions about the two most common safeguards we can trust—the one that places final authority in the church and the other that places final authority in the Bible. I'm just trying to be candid. If we're in search of the real God, we don't have to be afraid of reality.

IF WE'RE IN SEARCH OF THE REAL GOD, WE DON'T HAVE TO BE AFRAID OF REALITY.

Can we just say it? These approaches are limited. They are limited by the humanity of the humans who agree upon them and by the humanity of the humans who apply them. They are not foolproof. They don't confer as much safety as we might hope they would.

They are not without merit. They help. But the certainty we think they confer may be less sure than the certainty we seek.

THE PROBLEM OF "WHICH BIBLE?"

The challenge of interpreting the Bible sits on an even more fundamental question: which Bible are we interpreting?

Within the Bible itself there is no definitive list of the books that constitute the Bible. The issue was in dispute within the community of Israel during the lifetime of Jesus. One group recognized more writings as authoritative than did another. (Jesus seems to have sided with the group that included the wider selection of writings.)

To understand what books are included in the Bible, we turn to the consensus of the community that claims the Bible as its sacred text, even though the final authority in the second safeguard approach is the Bible itself.

That doesn't mean it's a hopeless morass. For better or worse, the messy process of history has delivered a Bible to us more or less intact. The differences between the Protestant Bible and the Catholic Bible (the apocrypha or deuterocanonical books accepted as Scripture by Catholics but not by Protestants) don't have much impact on either the story or the portrait of God.

Yes, there are recent discoveries of gospels other than the canonical gospels of Mathew, Mark, Luke, and John.[4] These other gospels include the Gospel of Thomas and the more recently discovered Gospel of Judas. I've read many of them along with the more widely accepted gospels of Matthew, Mark, Luke, and John. When you compare the view of Jesus in the four gospels despite differences between them, the portrait holds together. When you add the portrait of Jesus in these other gospels, the coherence breaks down.

It's obvious from reading the more recently discovered gospels that they are shaped by a fundamentally different view of the world than that of the canonical gospels. Many of them have been called Gnostic gospels because they have a negative view of the physical world that contrasts sharply with the canonical gospels.[5] In a sense, they are more spiritual and less earthy. The story they seem to be

---

4. The Word *canon* simply refers to a list of books considered to be authoritative by a given community. *Canonical gospels* refers to the gospels of Matthew, Mark, Luke, and John, which were circulating widely in the early church and accepted as containing the perspectives of the earliest eyewitnesses by the most influential Christian communities of that time.

5. Gnosticism is a religious movement of the second century marked by a view of the physical world as inherently evil.

telling is a different story. It's less the story of God coming into the good world he created to advance its repair and more the story of a spiritually enlightened one offering escape from a hopelessly corrupt world.

Ultimately, stories rise and fall on their own merit. Movies with the most popular actors and biggest marketing budgets may still be box-office flops. Independent films can surprise the analysts and make it big. A great deal still depends on their stories: Are they compelling? Are they explanatory? Do they help us make sense of the world? Are they transformative? Do they have the power to invite us in and change the way we live for the better?

J. B. Philips called this quality "the ring of truth."[6] Stories either have the ring of truth or they don't. The ones that do have a leg up on the ones that don't.

Who decides whether or not a story has the ring of truth? After all the recommendations from friends and family members and respected institutions, after all the swirl of critical acclaim or lack thereof, *you* do. You may be correct or incorrect in your decision. You may think you recognize "the ring of truth" and be mistaken. But it's up to you to decide. It has never been otherwise.

Elaine Pagels, one of the academics who popularized the Gnostic gospels, does a wonderful job describing the difference between the story told by the newly discovered Gnostic gospels and the story told by the gospels of Matthew, Mark, Luke, and John.

No one has ever accused Elaine Pagels of defending Christian orthodoxy. Her take on the differences between the Jesus of the

---

6. J.B. Phillips, *Ring of Truth: A Translator's Testimony* (Vancouver, BC: Regent College Publishing, 2004).

canonical gospels and the Jesus of the Gnostic gospels is not colored by a prior commitment to the validity of either telling. Her telling of the differences between the two, therefore, is itself telling: "The orthodox Christians saw Christ not as one who leads souls out of this world into enlightenment [the Gnostic view of Jesus] but as 'fulness of God' come down into human experience—into *bodily* experience—to sacralize it ['make it sacred']."[7]

The difference presents us with a choice: we have to choose the Jesus whose story has the ring of truth. As I compare the two stories, a Jesus who is a spiritual guru showing us another way to escape the physical world isn't nearly as good in the news department as a Jesus who represents a God coming into the good world to change the course of history from within history.

MAKING SENSE OF THINGS BEYOND OUR CULTURAL LENSES

Everything in the Bible doesn't make perfect sense to us in our context. That includes important things. Anyone who tells you otherwise is overselling.

Since the New Testament was written about two thousand years ago, the pace of change in the development of human culture has increased exponentially. Things presented in the Bible as self-evident, even things understood to be central, are not self-evident to us. Take, for example, the biblical understanding that Jesus died for our

---

7. Elaine Pagels, *Gnostic Gospels* (Phoenix: Orio, 2006), 146. See the entire conclusion for Pagels's full comparison of the Gnostic and the canonical vision of Jesus.

sins as a form of what is called by the specialists "substitutionary atonement."

Substitutionary atonement is the idea that Jesus' death on the cross was necessary to save us from our sins because God required a bloody sacrifice to atone for, or cover, or cancel, our sins. Someone had to pay, and God accepted the payment Jesus made "on our behalf." Substitutionary atonement requires an understanding of the bloody sacrifices that were offered in the temple by the priests of Israel "on behalf of" the sins of the nation as a whole and/or individuals. This practice, in turn, had historical roots in the even more ancient practices of many tribal peoples. Very early in human history, we seem to have come up with the idea that offering innocent life, signified in the bloodletting of an innocent living creature, effects something at the intersection of the human and the divine.

EVERYTHING IN THE BIBLE DOESN'T MAKE PERFECT SENSE TO US IN OUR CONTEXT.

As a brand-new disciple of Jesus, I heard people singing songs about the blood of Jesus covering our sins. I remember asking how this actually worked. To my mind, his blood fell on a piece of ground halfway around the world two thousand years ago, so the mechanism of its covering my sins was difficult to imagine. The answers I got didn't satisfy. I could accept that it was so, but only because enough other things about Jesus made sense to me.

Let's take a closer look at this problem. In certain respects, a God who humbles himself, taking the form of humanity even to the point of suffering and death, resonates with us perhaps even more than it did for the ancients. We like our leaders to be like us. We like them to drive ordinary cars and live in ordinary homes. We like it that Jeff Bezos outfitted his office at Amazon.com with a wood door turned into a desk just like everyone else at the company. That's our kind of billionaire.

Although the simple fact that Jesus suffered and died might not bother us, it did bother many in the ancient world. Especially to the ancient Jewish mind, a crucified Messiah was an oxymoron.

Sometimes the New Testament writers tackled this particular problem by framing the crucifixion in the familiar language of bloody sacrifices offered in the Jewish temple to atone for sin. (It's important to remember that this was not the only way they explained the meaning of Jesus' suffering and death.)

One can try to understand how the ancient Israelites experienced the bloody sacrifices offered on their behalf by their priests in the temple. Nevertheless, it is far removed from our frame of reference.

One can tell contemporary stories involving an innocent person "taking the punishment" of a guilty person, as when Maximilian Kolbe, a Catholic priest in the Nazi death camps, offered his own life in place of a Jewish prisoner. Stories like this have real power, and by telling them, the crucifixion as a substitution can make more sense to us, at least emotionally. But the examples beg the question, how does God fit into this? The story of Maximilian Kolbe's substitutionary sacrifice invites us to imagine God as a guard in the concentration camp.

If you're waiting for me to solve this conundrum with a brilliant and satisfying explanation of how substitutionary atonement makes perfect sense to people like us who are so far removed from the cultural experience of bloody sacrifice offered in temples by priests to effect something between the human and the divine, you will be disappointed. I can't do it.

I can say that for Jesus to have willingly offered himself as a bloody sacrifice for my sins is truly awe inspiring—such a love to pay such a price, assuming it was necessary. But why his bloody sacrifice would be necessary doesn't make sense to me in the way it made sense to those steeped in a tradition where these sacrifices were practiced.

I think it's important to listen to the perspectives of people in very different cultures than our own. If it applies in general, it applies especially in the case of the Bible. It's all too easy to dismiss something simply because it's foreign, but in doing that, we're assuming our cultural lenses are the only good lenses. That doesn't mean I can simply transport myself into another culture as though it were my own. Compared to the ancient peoples, the language of bloody sacrifice will always be a second language for me.

Having said that, something in the story of Jesus dying for my sins speaks to my modern abhorrence of the whole system of bloody sacrifice.

Jesus is presented in the New Testament as a high priest who ends the era of bloody sacrifice by offering *himself* (rather than the blood of rams, sheep, or turtledoves). He does so, not in the temple in Jerusalem, but "outside the camp" at a place called Golgotha, which was a toxic waste dump, what we might call a God-forsaken place. That was his "holy of holies," the place Jesus made holy by his bloody sacrifice to end all bloody sacrifices. A God who makes the God-forsaken places of this world holy speaks powerfully to me, especially when it brings the era of bloody sacrifices to an end.

In other words, there seems to be a development in the Bible on this issue of bloody sacrifice. God takes the preexisting and nearly universal practice of sacrifice and begins to shape it, to set boundaries around it, to channel it in certain directions through the law of Moses. He is willing to become involved in the process. He receives, even commissions sacrifices as a means to make atonement, or cover, or cancel the divine offense incurred by sins. By sacrificing himself, Jesus brings them to an end.

This suggests to me that *something* in my modern reaction against the idea that God would require bloody sacrifice isn't just modern rebellion against ancient tradition. I'm left with many unanswered questions. Was the idea of bloody sacrifice God's idea in the first place, or was it an accommodation to a nearly universal human instinct? The God of the Bible speaks in human languages. The languages were not his invention, but ours. By speaking in our language, he is accommodating himself to us. Was something like that going on with the issue of bloody sacrifice, God accommodating himself to what was once a nearly universal human impulse? I don't know.

A GOD WHO MAKES THE GOD-FORSAKEN PLACES OF THIS WORLD HOLY SPEAKS POWERFULLY TO ME.

Should I just chuck the whole business of bloody sacrifice as beneath my dignity or God's? It's tempting, but I think we lose something doing that. Our connection with the divine isn't just mediated by the part of our brain that does our analytical, logic-driven thinking. Our connection with the divine is also mediated by our limbic system, that part of the brain that processes human emotion, and even more primitive structures of the brain that generate our fight-or-flight response. It is sometimes called "the reptilian complex," because we share this structure with less developed creatures.

With my analytic brain function, I may not think I need someone like a priest to go into God's presence on my behalf to make sure it's safe.[8] I may not *think* that way,

I THINK WE'RE ALLOWED TO SAY, "THAT DOESN'T MAKE SENSE TO ME."

but if I'm honest with myself, I *feel* that way about God sometimes. My feelings may be wiser than my thinking. Who's to say? When I allow myself to acknowledge that feeling, the New Testament perspective about Jesus' offering himself on my behalf on the cross once and for all, makes perfect sense, or at least enough sense to approach God with a lot more confidence.

But for all that, I must admit that my analytic brain function still isn't satisfied with the earliest explanations of why Jesus had to die as my substitute. I think we're allowed to say, "That doesn't make sense to me." We're allowed, even expected, to do our own wrestling with the meaning of the suffering and death of Jesus in our very different cultural setting. Perhaps this is why Jesus said, "I have much more to say to you . . . When he, the Spirit of truth, comes, he will guide you into all the truth" (John 16:12–13). I think the Spirit is still coming, still leading us into all the truth.

---

8. The high priests of ancient Israel did this once a year to offer sacrifice for the whole nation on the Day of Atonement. They tied a rope around the priest's ankle so that if the sins of the nation exceeded the mercy of God that year, they could pull on the rope to drag out the corpse. When the high priest came out alive, everyone breathed a sigh of relief.

THE POWER OF STORY TO
CROSS CULTURAL DIVIDES

Perhaps this is why the core of the revelation isn't the doctrinal explanations but the story itself: stories have a unique capacity to speak to people in very different circumstances. The same great story can move us for very different reasons.

The New Testament has other ways of framing the meaning of the cross. This would be easy to miss, because one of the most popular forms of Christianity, evangelicalism, has done a wonderful job simplifying the gospel so people can grasp it for themselves as individuals. "The blood of Jesus covers my sins" or "Jesus died in my place (as a substitute)" is a major part of the message that has been popularized by the evangelical quadrant.

But the New Testament writers have other ways of understanding the cross than through the lens of bloody sacrifice. Paul speaks of the cross as a unique demonstration of God's strength manifest in weakness. The greatest strength is sometimes demonstrated in vulnerability.

The New Testament writers also view the cross through the lens of solidarity. In fact, this is a major theme in the New Testament understanding of Jesus' suffering and death. Jesus came as the "Son of man" to identify with us as completely as possible. Through him, God was entering into the human experience so that even at our most God-forsaken moments, we would not be alone. We suffer; he suffers. He dies; we die with him. He lets the full weight of suffering wash over him, and when it's past, he lives, and we live with him if we'll have him. Jesus isn't fundamentally a path of escape from suffering (though he often alleviates suffering) as much as a path through suffering to a new kind of life.

Suffering is *the* question of human existence. Other creatures suffer, but we are uniquely aware of our suffering. Like no other species in pain, we ponder its meaning. Why, in this wonderful world, must we suffer?

JESUS ISN'T FUNDAMENTALLY A PATH OF ESCAPE FROM SUFFERING . . . AS MUCH AS A PATH THROUGH SUFFERING TO A NEW KIND OF LIFE.

Biology has an answer, but it's a cold one. As novelist and poet Stephen Crane wrote, "A man said to the universe: 'Sir, I exist!' 'However,' replied the universe, 'the fact has not created in me a sense of obligation.'"[9] The same biology that offers this answer has also developed brains that inevitably search beyond the answer it offers. Back to square one: why?

Suffering is one of the unsolved mysteries of life, and it's one of the unsolved mysteries of the Bible. Just because we try to wring an answer to this puzzle out of the Bible doesn't mean the Bible must yield one.

Where is God when we suffer and die? That's the question the Bible speaks to. And the answer is: right next to us, just as Jesus suffered and died right next to the two robbers. The Bible portrays a God who is wounded by our suffering, who is involved in our suffering, and who, in the mystery of the cross, suffers with and for us. His passing through suffering and death into a new form of life gives us hope.

Just as important, the vision of Jesus suffering and dying has

---

9. Stephen Crane, "A Man Said to the Universe: 'Sir, I Exist!'" in *War Is Kind and Other Lines*, 21 (1899), http://www.linguatech.com/scrane/scrane10.htm#poem01 (accessed October 25, 2007).

enormous power to affect the way we relate to our fellow human beings when they suffer and die. Left to our own devices, we withdraw from the suffering of others. But the suffering and death of Jesus tells us to draw close to others in their suffering and dying. In his assessment of the historical factors behind the remarkable spread of Christianity in the first few centuries, sociologist Rodney Stark points out that during the plagues Christians were known for nursing the sick rather than abandoning them.[10]

HIS PASSING THROUGH SUFFERING AND DEATH INTO A NEW FORM OF LIFE GIVES US HOPE.

Surprisingly, Jesus didn't offer extensive explanations regarding the meaning of his impending suffering and death. For the most part, he made his way to the cross and invited us to follow. "If anyone would come after me, he must deny himself and take up his cross daily and follow me," he said (Luke 9:23 NIV). *Be willing to follow even if it means unto death* is what I understand him to mean.

If you want to be part of repairing the world, you had better summon your nerve. Jesus wasn't able to speak the truth he was given with such freedom until he settled something in his heart: *I don't care if this threatens the powers that be; I'm going to obey the Father come what may.*

Jesus' willingness to die for the truth was also God's willingness to die for us. We must do likewise if we're to serve the truth and the God he served for the sake of the world he loved.

---

10. Rodney Stark, *The Rise of Christianity* (Princeton, NJ: Princeton University Press, 1996), 82.

This message wasn't just aimed at individuals as a kind of spiritual tonic or balm for their sense of guilt over individual wrongs committed. In this individualism-run-amok culture, it's not a surprise that many Christians are focused on the death of Jesus as the solution to their individual sin problem. But it was also aimed at the nation of Israel, representing all people who would aspire to be God's people on earth, a city set on a hill, a light to the surrounding nations. Israel was, like so many nations, under the impression that the only option for dealing with enemies was to defend against them by violent means. This makes a great deal of sense and has for centuries been viewed as a morally acceptable response. It may still be. But the problem is, this morality rarely ends the cycle of violence that makes the world a miserable place. Jesus came to offer an alternative path: love your enemies, even to the point of death—yours, not theirs.

There are times when the only way to end the cycle of violence and actually repair the world is to follow in the footsteps of Jesus, which is a path that may lead to a cross or its cultural equivalent. We must be willing to speak up, to act, to stand for the truth, even if it means that in the process we're crushed by the powers that be— like the Reverend Dr. Martin Luther King Jr. and others of his order of courageous human beings were.

This is what Jesus did, and the crucifixion is evidence. The Roman Empire gave him its best shot and killed him. But mysteriously, yet also as a demonstrable fact of history, his willingness to accept death on the cross unleashed a cascade of events that eventually led to vast numbers of people in the Roman Empire changing their allegiance from Caesar to Jesus, and through him, to the God of Israel— this weak, vulnerable-to-evil God whom the powers that be held in such contempt. In the light of history, who conquered whom and how?

COMPLEXITY, SIMPLICITY, CERTAINTY

By now you may be wondering about the sheer complexity of the issues surrounding the Bible. In a world of ever-increasing complexity, we crave simplicity. This is the appeal of a more simplistic view of the Bible as an instruction manual for life. Such a view confers a comforting sense of certainty for many people.

If you feel well established on your pilgrimage, you may be annoyed by all this second-guessing. Why bring up all these complicated questions? Don't these kinds of questions undermine faith?

They do undermine a certain version of faith, but it's a version of faith that isn't convincing for many people. Go into any of the major chain bookstores and you will find a large section devoted to religion. You will find works of popular inspiration. But you will also find books by scholars of religion raising all these complicated questions. They used to be relegated to the libraries of academia, but no longer. The questions that were once only whispered in secret are now being shouted from rooftops.

There are many people of faith who don't bother with these questions. They either don't ask them of themselves, or they don't consider them valid questions in the first place. They may simply live in a portion of the world where these pesky questions haven't intruded. But someone they love is asking these questions. And the people outside of faith looking in are asking these questions. So yes, the questions are troubling. But sometimes, for the sake of others, if not ourselves, we have to trouble ourselves with troubling questions.

At one time, most practitioners of and inquirers into faith didn't realize there were so many different ways to approach the Bible, each approach with its attendant strengths and weaknesses.

They didn't realize that the gospels of Matthew, Mark, Luke, and John weren't the only ancient texts about Jesus calling themselves gospels. But now, fifteen minutes' browsing in your local bookstore opens up a set of questions that used to be tackled only by religious specialists.

THE QUESTIONS THAT WERE ONCE ONLY WHISPERED IN SECRET ARE NOW BEING SHOUTED FROM ROOFTOPS.

We are a simple Internet search away from knowing more than we ever wanted to know or could think to ask about these questions. The cat is out of the bag. Information is available to nonspecialists at a scale unimaginable even a few decades ago. Ready or not, here it comes—and with it, complexity.

To a growing body of people, the simple answers now seem simplistic, the certain answers less certain. It's understandably upsetting to those who are firmly attached to old-time religion. It's frightening. But that doesn't mean it's not happening.

We can't play religion like it's a game of pin the tail on the donkey. The blindfolds keep falling off. Like it or not, we are in the process of leaving behind a certain form of certainty. We can no longer blindly trust[11] some of the older forms of certainty that served us for so long. It's all right. If God is God, he's still God. We can't always get what we want. But if we try, as the Rolling Stones say, "you just might find, you get what you need."[12] I don't think we're promised the kind of certainty we want. We're only supplied with enough to get by.

---

11. That is to say, assume.

12. Mick Jagger and Keith Richards, "*You Can't Always Get What You Want*," Let It Bleed, 1969, Rare & OOP.

WE KNOW, BUT WE KNOW IN PART

There's a paradox when it comes to knowing God. The closer you get to knowing, the more you are in a position to know, the less you feel that you actually know. The more confident you become about certain things, the less confident you become about others, including your capacity to know. Some of those who have deep mystical experiences of God express this paradox. On the one hand, they speak as though they know, they've tasted, and they've experienced, but on the other, they speak as though God is unknowable. One of them wrote a book about the experience of God with the paradoxical title *The Cloud of Unknowing.*

Paul, one of the New Testament writers, said, "We know in part" (1 Cor. 13:9). We know enough to live on, but our knowledge is incomplete, partial. This perspective is even more impressive when you realize it came from a writer who was not cautious in the advance of an argument if he felt he was right.

This particular writer had firsthand experience with partial knowledge. Paul, formerly Saul, was an early persecutor of the Jesus movement until he realized that what he thought he knew—and what he understood to be rooted in biblical truth—was wrong. He also had the difficult experience of advancing perspectives on the meaning of the good news of Jesus that were not universally accepted by some of the closest friends of Jesus.

Religion, which is concerned with knowing what comes closer than anything else to being unknowable, raises the philosopher's question, *How do we know what we know?*

Ultimately, we may not know how we know what we know. We have theories. But try as we might, we can't lock our knowing down.

IF WE ARE LOVED BY ONE WHO DOES KNOW, IF WE ARE GIVEN ENOUGH CLARITY TO PROCEED WHEN THE TIME COMES, IT WILL BE ENOUGH TO MAKE OUR WAY.

What we have instead is a choice: to trust that we are loved or not, to trust that we will be given enough clarity to proceed when the time comes to draw one step closer. If we are loved by one who does know, if we are given enough clarity to proceed when the time comes, it will be enough to make our way. I think it's all we are really offered. It doesn't leave us feeling in charge of the situation, that's for sure. But maybe that's part of the point.

A MOSAIC OF UNDERSTANDING?

Anyone who is earnest about drawing one step closer to the center has to have *some* way of knowing how to proceed. Can we at least begin to understand what factors enter the equation of discerning the way forward on this pilgrimage? Yes. They are sacred Scripture, sacred community, sacred experience, sacred reason, and sacred Spirit. "In what order?" you ask. We'll get to that.

Sacred Scripture refers to the books of the Hebrew Bible that informed Jesus and the books of the New Testament that were left in the wake of the movement he generated.

Sacred community refers to the tradition of which Jesus was a part: the human community, the community of Israel, and the community of those he called to follow him. It refers to those who have gone before and those who are still here.

Sacred experience refers to the experiences of God and his world that convey reality in subtle, vivid, and powerful ways, including such things as visions and dreams and inner impressions of God. Jesus had such experiences and conveys them to us.

Sacred reason refers to the capacity by which we, in the image of God, make sense of things. Jesus was understood by the first generation of followers to embody the Greek concept of *logos*, which included reason and wisdom. "Come let us reason together" (Isaiah 1:18) is a line from God in the writings of the prophet Isaiah, a favorite book of Jesus.

Sacred Spirit refers to the Holy Spirit, the Spirit by which Jesus did his acts of power, spoke his words of truth, and, as a human being, was connected to God. The dying and rising of Jesus was understood to presage an outpouring of the spirit "on all flesh" that would extend the presence of God far and wide.

WE KNOW WE'RE ON THE RIGHT TRACK WHEN THE FRAGMENTS OF THE MOSAIC ARRANGE THEMSELVES IN SUCH A WAY AS TO REVEAL THE LIKENESS OF JESUS.

Now back to the question: in what order? As you might expect, some followers of Jesus place the priority on sacred Scripture. Others say, "Wait a minute, sacred Scripture only came about as the Scripture of a community, so sacred community has pride of place." Still others lean toward sacred Spirit, as the author of sacred Scripture. And so on.

I think "In what order?" isn't the most helpful question to ask for understanding the relationship between such hopelessly interrelated factors. Scripture is not direct-deposited into us. We *read* or *hear* or *listen to* Scripture through lenses or filters. It cannot be otherwise. The lenses are experience, reason, community, and Spirit. How can we separate actual Scripture from our reading of Scripture through these lenses? If we can't separate them through these lenses, what does it mean to say Scripture trumps reason, community, experience, and Spirit?

The actual experience of engaging God through the reading of Scripture is different than that. We read Scripture in the context of community, mediated through experience, aided by reason, and all of it bathed as much as possible in the Spirit. The relationship between all these factors is interdependent.

For example, when Jesus said, "If your eye causes you to sin, pluck it out," he did so assuming that his listeners were employing their reason to extract his meaning (Matt. 18:9 NKJV). He didn't say, "I don't mean that literally, because I don't believe self-mutilation will really help. Be willing to do whatever is necessary, within reason, to deal with whatever your undoing is. I'm using this very vivid image so that you don't just assume that 'within reason' means 'within my comfort zone.'" It's not helpful to say Scripture trumps reason, because our reading of Scripture depends on our use of reason.

With such interdependent factors, rather than thinking hierarchically, it's perhaps more helpful to think of the kind of order that emerges through a mosaic.[13] In this design, fragments are arranged in relation to each other in such a way as to form a beautiful image. You know you've arranged the fragments in the right relationship to each other when the image formed is beautiful.

At any given time, on any given issue, facing any given need for God to make himself known, we know we're on the right track

---

13. I am indebted to Stanley Grenz for his use of this image in *Beyond Foundationalism: Shaping Theology in a Postmodern Context* (Louisville, KY: Westminster John Knox, 2001).

when the fragments of the mosaic arrange themselves in such a way as to reveal the likeness of Jesus. We simply have to trust that when we see him, we'll recognize him, even if it takes a while.

RESOLVING THE DILEMMA

So what are we left with in the face of the dilemma of a paralyzing complexity on one hand and a plain simplicity on the other? Do we know too much to be certain of anything?

Here is the central claim of Jesus brand spirituality: we are left with a person, Jesus of Nazareth.

Persons have a wonderful way of combining complexity with simplicity. The most highly developed, well-regarded, deeply human people are the ones who are at the same time incredibly complex and beautifully simple. They surprise us from time to time because they are complicated; their complexity confounds our efforts to pigeon-hole them. But they are also recognizable because they hold together. They do things uniquely suited to their nature. They are simply themselves.

Persons know and can be known. Jesus of Nazareth knows and can be known. With some persons we can hope to arrive at or grow into a kind of relational certainty. We can know that we're known. We can know that we're loved. We can know that we won't be left high and dry.

This is the person the Scriptures bear witness to so that we may come to him.

JESUS BRAND SPIRITUALITY STUDY QUESTIONS: BIBLICAL DIMENSION

If you are discussing these questions in a group, you may want to refer to the Discussion Ground Rules for guidance. These can be found in the appendix.

1. The Bible can be an inspiring and intimidating book. What are the things about the Bible, as you understand it, that either inspire or intimidate you, or both?

2. What do you think of the idea that there is a common thread or unifying theme that runs throughout the Bible? What was your response to the author's attempt to tell the story of the Bible in five short acts [see pp. 135–44]? Did you find it helpful (or not) and if so, how?

3. Have you ever personally identifed with someone's story in the Bible? What was it, and how did it move you?

4. How do you think Jesus' understanding or treatment of Scripture differed from his contemporaries?

5. The author thinks that we've underestimated the power of story as a means to convey truth. What do you think about this perspective? How have stories helped you engage the truth in ways that other ways of truth-telling haven't?

6. What are your thoughts on the tension between the certainty we crave and the idea that our knowing is always partial, at best? Have you ever found yourself acknowledging less certainty than you once had concerning a matter of faith or spirituality?

COMMUNAL
DIMENSION

9

EVERYTHING ABOUT GOD
IS RELATIONAL

My nephew Danny suffers from autism, a condition that affects a person's ability to make connections. So it was especially poignant when I was wandering through a museum in New York City, the city of strangers, many of whom were cramped into a small space looking at various persons bereft of animating spirit, their bodies having been plasticized for anatomical display, to hear Danny sing out, "The more we get together, together, together, the more we get together, the happier we'll be." I heard the voice of God speaking through Danny, and it's not the first time.

Connections are the means by which God creates soul, I think. If this is part of the soul, then we've got some rethinking to do about religion in general and Jesus brand spirituality in particular.

If connections create soul, then being social or communal, and to what extent, isn't something we choose to do. It's what we are. Everything about God and everything about us, perhaps everything about all that is, is relational. And the sooner we realize it and act accordingly, the happier we'll be.

WHAT IS SOUL?

With the advance of the cognitive sciences, with its magnetic resonance imaging technology poking around in our inner depths, observing us in various states of communing with the divine, we cannot help but wonder where and whether and how the soul, if it is, is. When a person is meditating and a certain portion of brain lights up, is that soul? Or is soul invisible, undetectable? We know animals have emotions; some appear to have the beginnings of a moral sense. Do they have soul? If you are curious about questions like these, this is the time to be alive.

Pop religion has its own understanding of soul. Souls are immaterial entities existing before the foundation of the world and into eternity. When a child is conceived or shortly thereafter, one of these souls enters his or her body; when that body wears out, the soul is released to its previous unshackled state. Or so says pop religion.

Jesus brand spirituality has an earthier view of soul than that. The soul begins with the body. It may live on after death[1]—how or in what form we don't know—but it begins with body. As you

---

1. John Polkinghorne, a Cambridge professor of mathematical physics before he became an Anglican priest, thinks "soul" may be the information code that determines every person; when we die, God holds our code in memory until such time as it is to be reanimated. See Polkinghorne, *Quarks, Chaos, and Christianity* (New York: Crossroad, 1994), 93–94. Better yet, read the whole thing; it's a treat.

might expect, this understanding of soul begins in Genesis, the book of beginnings. Soul first appears with the creation of that mystery figure mysteriously named simply "the man" as though he represents "the human." "The LORD God formed the man from the dust of the ground and breathed into his nostrils the breath of life, and the man became a living being" (Gen. 2:7 NIV).

That word translated "being" is the Hebrew *nepes,* meaning that which breathes. It's the first appearance of the word *soul* in the book that informed Jesus. *Nepes,* that which breathes, is life, self, person, soul.

We don't have a soul in a body; we are body; we are soul.

In Genesis, the human became soul when a connection occurred with the other, the other being God. Connection creates soul. At that moment, the human might have opened his newly animated eyes and uttered, "You are, therefore I am."

WE DON'T HAVE A SOUL IN A BODY; WE ARE BODY; WE ARE SOUL.

Jesus brought into bold relief an understanding of God's being that had only been hinted at before, that God's own being is marked by connection. That God within his very God-ness is ongoing relationship.

The word for this is *Trinity.* God is a community of persons: Father, Son, and Holy Spirit. This language emerged after generations of reflection on the events described in the Gospels. But the seed of it is there in the Gospels. For example, as the prophet John baptizes Jesus, the Spirit descends in the form of a dove and a voice is heard, at least by Jesus, saying, "'This is my beloved Son, in whom I am well pleased" (Matt. 3:17 NKJV). In this moment, Father, Son, and Holy Spirit are present simultaneously, each distinguishable from the other yet profoundly connected.

What this says about Jesus is one thing, but the real shock occurs as we come to grips with what this says about God. God is irreducible relationship. Which means that everything about God and everything that comes from God is relational.

Nodal Points on a Network

We become soul in the same way a network becomes a network, by virtue of connections. The Internet is a network. As such, it is that web of connections that links computers to their progeny, servers, and to each other. One computer doth not a network make.

Each of us as a soul-being is like a nodal point on a network. We are distinct from others, taking up our own place on the network, but connected.

WE BECOME SOUL IN THE SAME WAY A NETWORK BECOMES A NETWORK, BY VIRTUE OF CONNECTIONS.

Soulful humanity craves connection. In the garden, even after God breathed into the human, it wasn't well with his soul. More connection was needed than existed. God said, "It is not good for the man to be alone" (Gen. 2:18). God connection is primary, but it necessarily leads to other connections. In the garden, humanity is connected with God, with others, and all living things; because these connections are well, we are well within ourselves. It is well with our soul.

If this understanding is correct, or at least part of the picture of soul, then any disruption of relationship anywhere on the network has the potential to affect the entire network. From a certain perspective, what goes on between you and God is nobody's business but your own. Except that it's everybody's business. We're all affected by each other. Anything that affects you, including God, affects me, however indirectly.

THE MYTH OF INDIVIDUALISM

This view of reality runs contrary to a powerful thread running through modern society in general and American culture in particular. I'm an American, which is supposed to mean I'm a fierce individualist. If so, I'm one of those fierce individualists who can exist only in a community. In fact, as a contemporary individual, I'm fiercely *dependent* on more people than perhaps any individual has been at any other time of history.

Pick one simple thing that I depend on—the gasoline to fuel my car that allows me to get to work and back. How many individuals are absolutely essential to locate the oil in the field, operate the drill, extract the crude, transport it to a refinery, and distribute it to the gas station in my neighborhood? You get the picture. Fiercely independent, that's me all right! Until I want to actually go somewhere or do something.

The American myth of individualism has empowered a great burst of entrepreneurial endeavors. There's something soul stirring and admirable in the picture it conjures of what it means to be human. It's an important counterbalance to the powerful nation-states of modern times. It even captures something of what it means to be made in the image of God. Each of us is some*one*. But our emphasis on the individual may have reached the point of diminishing returns.

Individualism and the story of independence it tells makes it difficult for us to appreciate how profoundly connected everything is to everything else. We struggle to grasp certain realities: that abject poverty in Africa must eventually have an impact on life in North America. Localized outbreaks of opportunistic disease become epidemics for lack of a decent public health system; all it takes is the right virus and the epidemic becomes a pandemic with a global reach. It's just a matter of time.

The American myth of individualism makes it difficult for us to mobilize the political will to deal with environmental threats, especially when the problems can only be understood as part of incredibly complex (interconnected) systems like the global climate. How could the carbon my car produces while driving impact the climate such that some people in low-lying areas will be flooded and others will suffer greater drought? Blinded by individualism, it's easier to believe that we're not actually that connected.

THE HARMFUL LOSS OF SOCIAL CONNECTIONS

Our failure to appreciate the importance of connections is coming back to haunt us. We feel it already in our loss of social connections. In *Bowling Alone: The Collapse and Revival of American Community*, sociologist Robert Putnam describes one of the most powerful negative influences on American society, a steep decline in what he calls "social capital."[2] Social capital consists of the connections we have with other people at work, at home, and in civic organizations, faith

---

2. Robert D. Putnam, *Bowling Alone: The Collapse and Revival of American Community* (New York: Simon & Schuster, 2001).

centers, community groups, extended family, and so on. He calls it "capital" because it is a form of wealth with measurable impact on health and well-being.

By all measures, social capital reached a zenith during the generation of those who fought World War II and then went on to build the modern highway system, communications system, and large corporations. Beginning with the baby boomers, social capital has been in precipitous decline. Each successive generation has less than the one before it. According to Putnam's extensive research, the impact is measurable and widespread, affecting increasing rates of depression, suicide, malaise, headache, gastrointestinal distress, and insomnia. The more we get together, the happier we'll be.

The title of the book *Bowling Alone* is drawn from an event that took place in Ypsilanti, Michigan, which is near my hometown, Ann Arbor. A man went into renal failure and needed a kidney. He was in a bowling league, and one of his bowling league buddies, someone he knew only from the bowling league, donated the kidney that kept him alive. Today, however, more of us are bowling alone.

At the end of the book, Putnam offers a five-point plan for reversing the decline of social capital. Putnam is writing as a secular scientist. Yet he includes in his prescription the need to foster a spiritual "great awakening."[3]

Putnam's follow-up book, *Better Together: Restoring the American*

---

3. Ibid., 409. Such awakenings—like the Great Awakening in the 1740s that helped end the British slave trade and the Second Great Awakening that fueled the American abolitionist movement—are one of a few factors that have demonstrably reversed decline in social capital in the past.

Community, is a case study on communal structures or movements that are effectively reversing the decline in social capital today.[4] One of the groups studied is Saddleback Community Church, a mega-church in California that intentionally fosters community through facilitating participation in small groups, whether recovery groups, Bible studies, or affinity groups organized around shared interests.

GROUP AVERSION

I suffer from something afflicting many us: group aversion. I distrust groups. I spent my childhood in classrooms crowded with too many baby boomers, stood in too many lines waiting for something to happen, and rode my bike through neighborhoods with too many houses of exactly the same dimensions and construction materials.

Left to my own inclinations, I might easily maintain a close friendship or two and connect with those family members with whom I enjoy a relatively stress-free relationship. Even then, as a middle-aged man, I would be slightly ahead of the game. But my social capital would be low.

I was driven by abject need to reach out to others beyond my natural social preferences. Having gotten married right out of high school as a teenage parent, I was in a high-risk marriage. It was just the three of us in our married student apartment on campus. My wife and I had only two friends in town, Mark and Dan. We had two sets of parents forty-five minutes away. Scattered siblings busy with their own lives rounded out the social capital. It wasn't

4. Robert D. Putnam, *Better Together: Restoring the American Community* (New York: Simon & Schuster, 2003).

enough. I was stressed, my wife was depressed, and we needed some more support.

A graduate student in engineering named Jonathan, raised in Kerala, India, invited Nancy and me to a Bible study. Having just begun to read the Bible in earnest, I was curious to learn from others but wary of the idea of walking into a living room full of strangers. We went.

As fate would have it, the group was studying an obscure text from one of Paul's writings, having to do with the importance of women wearing head coverings "because of the angels" (1 Cor. 11:10). A respected scholar who holds a very high view of Scripture, a respected Pentecostal theologian as a matter of fact, unafraid to embrace practices outside the cultural mainstream, has said that there is virtually no hope of understanding what Paul meant by this text.[5] The participants in the group voiced various opinions about the text, offering thoughts on what Paul meant and why. Most of the people in the group seemed to think the wearing of head coverings by women was a good idea and a wonderful way to express one's devotion to God. Each of the opinions offered stretched credulity. I couldn't believe there were people alive in the (then) twentieth century who had such conversations.

After returning from the Bible study, Nancy and I looked at each other and burst out laughing. It was 1971. The campus of the University of Michigan was throbbing with antiwar activism. Feminism was on the rise. Nancy wasn't in the habit of wearing a bra, let alone head coverings!

---

5. Gordon D. Fee, *The First Epistle to the Corinthians*, New International Commentary on the New Testament (Grand Rapids: Eerdmans, 1987), 521.

"Should we go back?" I asked.

"I'd like to," Nancy replied. "Some of their ideas were goofy, but there was a lot of love in that living room."

Since then, we've tended to look past the goofy ideas and look for the love in the living room. At least enough love to accept an opinion like, "Whatever Paul meant, I think we all have bigger fish to fry than figuring out what the angels had to do with Paul's wanting the women to cover their heads; can we move on to the next verse?"

LEARNING LABORATORIES OF LOVE

Jesus brand spirituality is a path that leads beyond individualism toward community. Community is where we practice the skills of cooperation—of love, mutual respect, forbearance, conflict resolution, forgiveness, the balance between stating our own needs and taking concern for the needs of others.

Jesus is in the business of forming such communities. He came to form a movement, a social network, a corporate enterprise organized around his teaching and empowered by his presence. The Greek word for such communities is *ecclesia* (translated "church"), meaning "called out" or "gathered ones." It is derived from the ancient Greek city-states in which citizens would be called out to gather in the public square to handle communal business.

JESUS BRAND SPIRITUALITY IS A PATH THAT LEADS BEYOND INDIVIDUALISM TOWARD COMMUNITY.

Jesus prepared his first disciples to participate in these communities by giving them a new commandment: "you must love one another" (John 13:34). The New Testament writings have about forty such sayings, including "love one another," "forgive one another," "correct one another," and "bear with one another." Communities that formed around a shared commitment to Jesus become laboratories where these sayings are practiced.

It's not a picnic. Or if it is, there's plenty of potato salad sitting out in the sun too long. These communities are not the perfect family you always dreamed of. From the earliest times, these communities achieved mixed results. At times, they almost seemed to be little conclaves of heaven on earth; at other times, judging from the earliest records, they were racked with dissension and conflict.

WHERE WE PRACTICE THE REPAIR MECHANISM

The Jesus communities were never conceived of as utopias. They are learning laboratories of forgiving love. They are messy places where we make mistakes in relating to others and practice the repair mechanism that Jesus stressed so heavily in his teaching.

If, as soul-beings, we are nodal points on a network composed of connections, then our well-being depends on learning to repair the damage done to the connections by acts of misunderstanding, injustice, unkindness, hostility, and selfish inconsideration. The primary repair mechanism is forgiveness.

Jesus made forgiveness the centerpiece of the prayer that was to mark his movement. "This, then," he said, "is how you should pray:

'Our Father in heaven,/ hallowed be your name,/ your kingdom come,/ your will be done,/ on earth as it is in heaven./ Give us today our daily bread./ And forgive us our debts,/ as we also have forgiven our debtors./ And lead us not into temptation,/ but deliver us from the evil one'" (Matt. 6:9–13).

Our Father, the first words of his prayer. *Deliver us from the evil one,* the last.[6] And in the middle, *Forgive us our debts as we also have forgiven our debtors.*

Forgiveness is a major theme in the Jesus path that leads away from evil. It's part of what delivers us from evil, including the wrongs we have done and the wrongs done to us.

Jesus highlighted the importance of forgiveness by this pointed commentary immediately following his sample prayer: "For if you forgive men when they sin against you, your heavenly Father will also forgive you. But if you do not forgive men their sins, your Father will not forgive your sins" (Matt. 6:14–15 NIV).

FORGIVENESS IS A MAJOR THEME IN THE JESUS PATH THAT LEADS AWAY FROM EVIL.

In another place, Peter asks how many times the same offender must be forgiven—as many as seven times? Jesus replies, "I tell you, not seven times, but seventy-seven times" (Matt. 18:22)—his way of saying, "A lot more than you'd ever consider reasonable."

---

6. The familiar closing line—"For thine is the kingdom, the power and the glory for ever and ever, amen"—is widely recognized as a later addition, and not in the original documents.

FORGIVENESS: A COMMUNAL ARRANGEMENT

What exactly is forgiveness? Though forgiveness involves the heart, including the emotions and the will, it can be thought of as a communal arrangement. It's a pattern of relating that is reinforced within a culture. We learn to forgive by being in a culture that values forgiveness as a social repair mechanism and provides a context of meaning for the practice of forgiveness.

Some cultures don't value forgiveness nearly as much as vengeance and retribution. They don't tell stories in which conflict is resolved by forgiveness. They don't have rituals that reenact forgiveness. Forgiveness may even be viewed as a sign of weakness, akin to the abject subordination of a dog rolling on his back with his paws in the air in the presence of a dominant animal. Or it may be viewed as something only a person in a position of power can practice as a sign of overwhelming strength, as if to say, *I'm so powerful that your harmful actions can't hurt me.*

Reinforcing forgiveness as a repair mechanism was a big part of Jesus' social agenda for ancient Israel. The people of Israel were oppressed by foreign occupiers who were constantly taking advantage of them. There were various strategies for overcoming the evil of this form of oppression: cooperating with the evil occupiers to gain personal advantage, living in remote communities away from the reach of the occupation forces, and overthrowing the occupiers by violent means. Jesus offered a different path of deliverance from the evil of enemies: love of enemies through the practice of forgiveness. He had a strategy to introduce forgiveness into the fabric of the culture: teach it, model it, and form little communities to spread it.

In the Middle East today, it's obvious that forgiveness is not a powerful repair mechanism between parties in continual conflict. Forgiveness doesn't have cultural currency as a response to enemies or people who have caused harm. What new possibilities might emerge if a leader like Gandhi or Martin Luther King Jr. or Desmond Tutu emerged from within the social movements of the Middle East?

JESUS COMMUNITIES ARE MEANT TO BE PLACES WHERE FORGIVENESS IS VALUED, MODELED, AND ENCOURAGED.

Jesus communities are meant to be places where forgiveness is valued, modeled, and encouraged as the way to respond to the harm we do to others and the harm others do to us. Wherever such communities are found, they are meant to serve as learning laboratories of forgiving love for the sake of the societies in which they are imbedded.

THE FLAKY RELATIVES PROVE IT'S A FAMILY

I learned something from Dick Bieber, the pastor who was talking to my dad when he came out of his coma. Dick decried what he called "churchianity." By "churchianity," he didn't mean church. Dick was knee-deep in the church enterprise, and as hard as he worked, he seemed to be having the time of his life. By "churchianity," I think he was trying to describe the tendency we have to gather with the pleasantly like-minded, the pleasantly healthy, the pleasantly homogenous groupings that we all naturally self-select, and to call whatever that is "church," as though it were the real deal.

Dick had friends who were like-minded, who enjoyed talking about the kinds of books and movies he enjoyed—just different enough to be interesting but not so different as to be *work*. Dick had a life, or at least he aimed at having one. But he didn't trust groups who called themselves churches but looked for all the world like what happens when birds of a feather flock together. Dick wanted it spicy. He wanted people from the Cass Corridor, Detroit's skid row, to be part of the church family. He wanted people who mumble to themselves and gesture oddly to be welcome.

ULTIMATELY, THE JESUS COMMUNITY IS NOT A PLACE FOR US UNLESS IT'S A PLACE FOR ALL OF US.

Dick wanted those people, considered odd by many, but "refreshing" by Dick, *and* the professors from Wayne State University, and the auto executives who drove in from the Detroit suburbs, and the people active in Boy Scouts and Girl Scouts and the PTA. He wanted to see what kind of magic happened when all those people coalesced in the hopes of taking one step closer to becoming the city that has no street names, the "beloved community" that filled the dreams of Martin Luther King Jr. and others.

I was once a leader in a religious community that was in many ways a taste of heaven on earth. We had Catholics and Protestants of various stripes and people like myself who preferred to be called simply "Jesus freaks"—all still part of their own churches, mind you, but also coming together in this ecumenical community. I received a lot. I gave a lot. I learned a lot.

When we said *community*, we weren't messing around. At one

time Nancy and I lived in a communal household that included our three children, a dog, and eight single people. We ate meals together, did chores together, and tried not to take long showers.

There were some frustrating moments. We used to have morning prayers in the basement. One morning I was the last to come down for morning prayers. Like everyone else, I had to come through the kitchen to get to the basement. And there in the kitchen I saw a pile of dog droppings that was not particularly fresh. Every one of my dear communal household members had left that for the next guy, and I was the last guy.

The part of that experience in that ecumenical community that I really regret was the time when we the leaders took this beautiful thing that God had created and tried to protect it by saying it was only for certain kinds of people. People who could fit in. People who wouldn't be too much of a drain.

The community that forms in the wake of Jesus isn't what it was meant to be unless there's a fair sampling of humanity represented. There have to be enough people who have it enough together to have a something that survives. But it has to have "refreshing" people too. Enough to be a learning laboratory for the one thing necessary: love.

And this is not just for the sake of the "refreshing" ones. It's for the sake of all of us. Because ultimately, the Jesus community is not a place for us unless it's a place for all of us. And we can't learn to be ourselves or believe that we're accepted as the selves we are unless we're accepting some others in spite of some things.

The flaky relatives, and we might be one of them, prove it's a family.

10

ALL YOU NEED IS LOVE,
PROPERLY UNDERSTOOD

Religion is a big field full of important questions, competing answers, controversies, and conundrums about which arguments are advanced, boundaries set, adherents sought, and opponents opposed. Thus it has been and will be for the foreseeable future.

Developments in neuroscience suggest that the human brain is biologically driven to be religious. As soon as our brains were able to consider potential dangers and threats in the abstract and be aware of the inevitability of suffering and death, we started working overtime on solutions; religion is one of the main things we either made up or discovered.[1]

Maybe that's why this part of being human can seem so fraught, so overwrought, and so inevitable. It's not just part of this or that particular culture from which we might hope to extract ourselves to

---

1. Andrew Newberg, Eugene D'Aquili, and Vince Rause, *Why God Won't Go Away: Brain Science and the Biology of Belief* (New York: Ballantine, 2002), 133–40.

get a break. It's part of *us*. If we didn't have any religion, we would be powerfully driven to find one, or if need be, to start one. Even our efforts to free ourselves from religion may be part of our religious quest. Perhaps we can't even back away from any particular religion without backing into another one. Oy vey!

Jesus didn't rise above the field of religion. He doesn't offer a nice and easy spirituality that allows us to sidestep all the tough issues and hard choices that come with making our way through the world. I wish I could report otherwise. I wish I could point you to an "easy does it" Jesus who found a way to rise above religion. I'm afraid that isn't possible, though, because Jesus isn't about to rise above us. He's here in the mess with us, and he's here for the long haul.

JESUS DIDN'T RISE ABOVE THE FIELD OF RELIGION.

What Jesus did is show us a way to be human that includes being religious. A way of being human that seeks out meaning and purpose and the connections between things and people and other living things and heaven and earth and events and God. What to pursue and what to ignore and what to flee. Who to be. How to be. Where to be.

We humans are able to follow anyone or anything only one step at a time. We're not called to wrap our arms around the world but to make our way through the world. We are pilgrims here.

While this doesn't exempt us from all the complexity of religion, it does clarify or simplify the endeavor. We're pilgrims. Our most pressing concern as pilgrims is taking one step closer. I, for one, appreciate the narrow focus of that. I think it's part of the package Jesus offered when he said, "My yoke is easy and my burden is light" (Matt. 11:30). When faced with the inevitable mess of religion, knowing I can't simply rise above it, I find rest for my soul when I remember that. *What's the next step closer to knowing that I can take with Jesus?*

What's the one thing we could say about God if our frame of reference for understanding God were Jesus? Careful, there's a lot at stake with a question like this. The answer to such a question could become a guiding light for your pilgrimage. Answer well.

WHAT'S THE ONE THING WE COULD SAY ABOUT GOD IF OUR FRAME OF REFERENCE FOR UNDERSTANDING GOD WERE JESUS?

My answer after nearly forty years of following (more or less, assuming fits and starts count) is this: God is love, properly understood. I hope the unoriginality of this doesn't disappoint you, but I think there's more to this than meets the eye.

God is love, properly understood.

GOD IS LOVE

If this statement, recorded in a letter written by John, the beloved disciple[2] (1 John 4:8) were written in the context of any other movement, it might be possible to understand it in the normal sense: that God is loving. But I think this was written more carefully than that.

---

2. Or, at least, this letter was written by someone in the community of which John, the beloved disciple of Jesus, participated.

Jesus understood himself to be Son in some very significant sense. As a fully human being, it's possible this awareness dawned on him as any deep awareness dawns on any of us. It came to him as he wrestled with his sacred Scriptures within his community, informed by his experience and reason, and by the Spirit who seemed at times to haunt him. I don't think he was born with this understanding or arrived at it early in his life. Like the rest of us, Jesus had to grow in wisdom and understanding.

As Son, Jesus understood himself to be in the closest possible communion with the one he called Abba, Father. As in, *one with*. It's clear that this Father was understood by him to be God. And as Son, he felt himself to be filled with and empowered by one he called Spirit, similarly divine.

Certainly the movement that Jesus spawned came in time to understand God differently than people did before Jesus came along. They came to understand that God is love, within himself. God is love, with the emphasis on *is*, and with the explicit understanding that *is* is meant in the most literal sense.

God *is* love because God is, within himself, irreducible, loving relationship. A Father ever generating love. A Son ever receiving and reciprocating love. And, as Augustine said, the love between them so intense as to be personed in the ever generated and generating Spirit.[3]

This is the answer to the question, What is the fire in the equations by which the universe came into being?

---

3. Notice that John 16:13 breaks the rules of grammar to emphasize the personhood of the Holy Spirit: "When the Spirit [neuter noun] comes, he [personal pronoun, breaking grammar rule] will lead you into all truth."

PROPERLY UNDERSTOOD

Jesus himself is the properly understood part. To understand Jesus is to properly understand love and the reality that God is love.

Understanding is an important word connected to a deep human need. I want to be understood. I don't want to be put in a category, and even less do I want to be mastered, like a phone number that's been memorized. I want to be understood.

I *like* people who go to the trouble of understanding me. I like people who ask me questions and listen carefully to the answers. I like people who stick with me and accept the contradictions that constitute me and appreciate the good things and put up with or lovingly confront the bad things. (At least I *want* to like those people.)

TO UNDERSTAND JESUS IS TO PROPERLY UNDERSTAND LOVE AND THE REALITY THAT GOD IS LOVE.

It's a lot of work to understand someone. A lot of time and effort go into the simple art of not jumping to conclusions about someone. A lot of quieting of your own quick thoughts about a person's motives is required, for example. A lot of paying attention is required.

My wife, Nancy, works harder than anyone I know to understand me, and do I appreciate it! Sometimes I'm working on a sermon and tell her what I'm thinking about saying before I know what it is myself; I string together some words in the vicinity of the thought, and Nancy just looks at me and says, "Spit it out, Wilson!" I know she's trying to understand me, which usually helps me to understand myself.

Jesus would like to be understood by us. The Gospels record some painful conversations between Jesus and people who are not going to enough trouble to understand him. You can just tell that it bothers him. It hurts him as it hurts us.

All these years of trying to follow Jesus won't have amounted to much if I haven't come to understand him better in the process . I think it would be quite possible, temptingly possible, to settle for something less than trying to understand him. I could settle for putting a great deal of my religious energy into mastering the version of Christian orthodoxy that most appeals to me, locking down all the most correct opinions on all the hot topics. And I could think that by so doing, I am understanding Jesus. But I don't think it works that way.

I believe that the process is more intensely and maddeningly personal than that. Jesus might wish to reveal something about himself that is other than my need to have a particular correct position on some perplexing issue of intense interest. He might be waiting for me to understand that certain something about him before I am capable of understanding his perspective on that other thing that has me all wound up.

Understanding Jesus is a different process than mastering Christianity. Jesus, being a person, is a subject, not just an object. Objects—like systems—can be mastered, but persons want to be understood, known, loved.

God is love, properly understood. Persons are also more than the sum of their parts, more than even the most accurate list of their attributes. The New Testament writer Paul took a stab at listing the attributes of love:

> Love is patient, love is kind. It does not envy, it does not boast, it
> is not proud. It is not rude, it is not self-seeking, it is not easily

angered, it keeps no record of wrongs. Love does not delight in evil but rejoices with the truth. It always protects, always trusts, always hopes, always perseveres. (1 Cor. 13:4–7 NIV)

It was a valiant effort on Paul's part to describe love in that way. Inspired, even. It was humble of Paul, since from what we can glean about his personal-relational skills, he probably struggled like we all do in putting some of these aspects of love into practice. But as good an effort as it was, it proves the point: love is meant to be embodied more than it's meant to be described. To understand

UNDERSTANDING JESUS IS A DIFFERENT PROCESS THAN MASTERING CHRISTIANITY.

love, you have to meet love in a person. Love in a person fills in all the gaps left between our best descriptions, and some of the love that comes out in the gaps surprises us.

But persons are particular as is God if God is love. God is not some*thing*: Love. God is some*one*: Love.

Now comes the unpleasant part.

ALL YOU NEED IS LOVE

Every religion has its ascetics, people who choose to live stripped-down lives. Some of these people seem pretty extreme. Like the Christian ascetics who were called "pillar saints" (or stylites) because they sat for days (even years!) on the top of long poles to practice their asceticism. We think of ascetics as people who refuse to bathe or shave or use good hygiene. We think of them as people we wouldn't want to be around.

We who don't live stripped-down lives tend to resent ascetics, especially when they depend on donations from people like us so that they can practice their simplicity. What earthly good are such people? Sometimes the mere presence of ascetics makes us feel vaguely guilty: *Maybe I don't really need as much as I think I do.* That ascetics are connected to religion may even be part of what gives religion a bad name in our estimation.

The fact that every religion has its ascetics, though, is something we should pay attention to. John the Baptist, the prophet who made way for Jesus of Nazareth, was an ascetic. Jesus went through periods when he practiced ascetic disciplines like fasting and prolonged solitude. (Though he was also criticized for eating and drinking.)

ANY RELIGION THAT SEEKS TO CONNECT US WITH WHAT IS ULTIMATE MUST NECESSARILY ALSO STRIP US OF THOSE THINGS THAT ARE UNNECESSARY.

What is it these people are getting at that deserves our attention? They get at the reality that any religion that seeks to connect us with what is ultimate must necessarily also strip us of those things that are unnecessary, or unhelpful, or whose proximate goodness keeps us from an ultimate one.

All you need is love, properly understood, is saying the same thing. Jesus brand spirituality is a path that promises to strip us of all that is not love, no matter how painful that may be, no matter how severe or exacting that may seem to us. This tends to separate those who want love on love's terms from those who only want love on their own terms, which is to say, those who don't want love.

Jesus once said, "Wide is the gate and broad is the road that leads to destruction, and many enter through it. But small is the gate and narrow the road that leads to life, and only a few find it" (Matt. 7:13–14). Narrow, because eventually the only thing allowed in the center of the fire of love is love. We get to go there without being pure love ourselves; we get to be loved by love, even when we bring a considerable amount of unlove into love's presence. But we only get to stay there if we're willing to have all that is not love stripped away by love. Eventually.

God is love, properly understood. And all you need is love, properly understood.

The outward forms of asceticism are not required of all of us, thankfully. Many of us couldn't do it. Many of us shouldn't do it. Many more of us wouldn't want to do it if we could. I won't ask for a show of hands. But the thing about love to which ascetics bear witness is unavoidable: for love to have its way means we have to be willing to have everything that is not love stripped away from us. And love gets to decide what that is and what that isn't.

This means that the path of Jesus brand spirituality is littered with hard things: hardships, hard choices, hard decisions, hard times.

If you're doing comparison shopping, factor in all the hard things that come with every path, especially the hidden or deferred hard things that come with every so-called easy path. The Buddha had it right when he said all life involves suffering; this is a biological fact.

I once met a man who came from a country that was known for mistreating Christians. I said to him, "It must be hard to be a

GOD IS LOVE, PROPERLY UNDERSTOOD. AND ALL YOU NEED IS LOVE, PROPERLY UNDERSTOOD.

Christian in your country!" He just smiled at me as though I were the soft-headed neophyte that I was, and said, "It's hard to be *human* in my country! And in yours too!"

So don't make that mistake. Don't make the mistake of pursuing Jesus brand spirituality as a way to avoid hard things.

DON'T MAKE THE MISTAKE OF PURSUING JESUS BRAND SPIRITUALITY AS A WAY TO AVOID HARD THINGS.

You'll become frustrated and disillusioned. You'll feel rather foolish, and I would spare you that.

LOVE IS ALL YOU NEED

In that shimmering moment when young people streamed to Haight-Ashbury in San Francisco and danced in the park and gave out flowers—before the food ran out and the tourists came to take pictures and the drug dealers took over and it all came crashing down in the Summer of Love—there was a feeling that love might just break into the human experience and take over.

Jesus brand spiritually is more than that feeling, but it's not less than that feeling.

There's an extraordinary passage in one of the New Testament writings that says, "God is love. Whoever lives in love lives in God, and God in him. In this way, love is made complete among us so that we will have confidence on the day of judgment, because in this world we are like him. There is no fear in love. But perfect love drives out fear, because fear has to do with punishment. The one who fears is not made perfect in love" (1 John 4:16–18 NIV).

This is one of those passages that gives people in my line of work job security. This is a passage so dangerous, so out on the edge of cherished religious sensibilities, that people will always be looking for ways to explain it away so it doesn't undermine those sensibilities.

Take fear, for example. A great deal of religion trades in the currency of fear.

Groups are held together by creating boundaries that its members are afraid to cross. Religious groups seem to be particularly adept at this. Casting off fear might mean casting off restraint, which might mean everything falls apart and chaos ensues, just like it did when the hippies streamed into San Francisco in 1967. I don't have any answer to that legitimate fear of religion stripped of fear.

Or take punishment as another example. "Perfect love drives out fear, because fear has to do with punishment." That's a scary thought. Many people in this world don't do some very bad things because they fear the bad consequences of doing such bad things. I don't want them letting go of that fear. I worry about some of the things I might let myself do were it not for the rather ignoble fear of getting caught.

EVERYTHING THAT IS NOT LOVE WILL BE PURGED. EVEN FROM THINGS WE HOLD DEAR, LIKE OUR RELIGION.

I'm not doing a very good job of explaining this passage, am I? I bring it up because I think it's an example of the severity implicit in the statement "God is love, properly understood." God is love, and everything that is not love will be purged. Even from things we hold dear, like our religion.

Try another thought experiment. What if you knew that 20 percent of the things you believe with all your heart about God or the ways of God or the things of God were wrong? You didn't mean them to be wrong. You just misunderstood and got things wrong. If that's hard to imagine, try 10 percent. For those of you gifted with extraordinary self-confidence, try 5 percent. It's not an unreasonable possibility, given what we know to be true about the human condition. Need further convincing? Consider all the things that people in ages past thought that turned out to be wrong, including people who were more devoted to God than you are.

It would be fine if you were also told what those mistaken beliefs were so you could ditch them and feel better about what remained. But you're not told, or if you are, the message hasn't gotten through yet. In the meantime you just have to live with the knowledge that it's so. I don't know what the percentage is, but I cannot believe anything other than that there is a percentage, and it's greater than zero.

If I believe that God is love, properly understood, then I must be prepared to let go of anything once I'm convinced that it is not love. Anything. Even things that seem very sacred to me.

I think the people who originally decided to follow Jesus were people who were willing to do just that. I think Jesus selected them. Or he influenced them to become those kind of people. I picture Jesus saying something like this to them and to us: *You say you want love? Those of you who really mean it can have it.*

11
PILGRIMS' PARTING

The closing story in Luke's gospel is a story of pilgrims meeting and parting with the hopes of meeting again. It's the oddest story of pilgrimage in a library full of them, a story of pilgrimage with more loose ends than tied ones. As if it's a story that is making room for other stories—the loose ends waiting for other loose ends in the hope of forging connections. Perhaps with your story.

It begins on the evening of the first day of the new week, a grief-stricken evening for those following the last days of Jesus' life. Confusing rumors are already circulating of strange appearances of the deceased.

Two travelers are going nowhere in particular. If they are pilgrims, they are disoriented ones. They are traveling from Jerusalem, ordinarily the pilgrims' destination, to another place, Emmaus, a place that seems to have been selected because it was as good as any other. Sound and feel familiar?

A third person approaches along the way and strikes up a

conversation. A stranger to the others, he asks about the recent events that everyone in Jerusalem was talking about: a prophet in whom great hopes had been placed meeting an unhoped-for end.

The two are incredulous that the third has not heard of these things. They tell the sad tale, their brains addled by the cotton stuffing of grief.

The stranger in turn tells his own tale, beginning with the shared story of Moses and the prophets, laced throughout with the plaintive cry of the voices who composed the Psalms, winding his way through the story of Israel, the story of God in search of humanity, making connections unnoticed before, highlighting twists in the plot heretofore hidden.

The stranger's story resonates with the aimless pilgrims. No, it burns. It sears its way into the place where stories either make sense or they don't. This one makes sense as no other before it.

The story draws them in together. They feel connected to each other in grief and in newfound hope. They feel strangely connected to the storytelling stranger.

The sun is setting as they approach their destination. The stranger signals his intention to continue on his way. The thought of parting fills the pilgrims with a sadness beyond reckoning, as if all the sorrows of every parting were packed into this one. They implore the stranger to stay with them. "The day is nearly over and the night is falling," they say. "Please stay."

He agrees. They find an inn with a dinner table and sit down together.

The stranger takes the bread as was the custom, lifts it before them, and offers thanks. In that moment it's as if a stray shaft of eternity penetrates their hearts, and they recognize him. With that, he disappears from their sight.

But the parting doesn't crush them, because he left hope behind to energize them. And they were overjoyed and went back to Jerusalem at once to tell the others, some of whom had their own strange experiences to tell.

The experiences and the telling of them continues to this day. A story too good to be true or too good not to be?

You decide.

But how do you decide?

That's for you to decide too.

There was a time when people expected to be told how and when they were to decide. *Here's how it works. All or none. Take it or leave it.* The authorities framed the decision and the process for making the decision.

We don't depend on the authorities like we used to. It's not just that we don't like to be told what to do; it's that we don't trust the authorities to know better necessarily.

I know that sounds appealing, but it's also confusing. Because the problems we face involve a level of complexity few of us can master. Food appears in the grocery store, and many of us are not sure exactly how it got there or where it came from. Scientists tell us things about reality that we have no way to verify for ourselves. We depend on technologies whose internal functioning we can't hope to fathom. When it's time to set my watch for daylight saving time, I hand it to my daughter because she's the expert.

WE DON'T DEPEND ON THE AUTHORITIES LIKE WE USED TO.

So it's not that we don't need experts or wouldn't benefit by having a few trusted ones around. It's that we know too much to hand them the car keys like we used to.

I'm an authority, and I can feel the shift. I stand up week after week and speak to people who have gathered in search of the treasure buried in the field of religion. I may be a witness. I may be a fellow traveler. But I am no longer the expert. Like religious authorities of the past, I am not better educated than those who listen week after week. I don't have a bigger library. The people who sit in the chairs listening while I stand talking

THERE'S A PROGRESSION IN THE UNFOLDING STORY OF GOD IN SEARCH OF HUMANITY. . . IT'S A PROGRESSION FROM THE FEW TO THE MANY.

know that they are only a few mouse clicks away from knowing many of the things I know about the study of God. I can't trace my authority through an unbroken chain of authorities laying hands on successive generations going back to Jesus himself. There are too many gaps in the record to settle the claims and counterclaims anymore.

There is no Moses come down from the cloud-covered mountain with tablets in his hands to tell us which end is up. There is just the cloud and our curiosity and our need and our experiences and our longings.

There's a progression in the unfolding story of God in search of humanity. It's a progression that Jesus was very involved in advancing. It's a progression from the few to the many.

Once upon a time, the weight of responsibility, the burden of leadership, rested upon a relative few. The few went up on the mountaintop and had visions of God and came down to tell the rest of us.

Moses went by himself to the mountaintop, met God, and came down. But Jesus took some of his friends with him. And then later, the cloud that they entered together took him away beyond their sight only to descend again on 120 of them as the beginning of the end when the Spirit would come "on all flesh" (Acts 2:17 NKJV).

This is such a big adjustment in the way we do religion that two thousand years later we're still catching up. Religion is catching up with God.

WE SHOULD BRISTLE LESS AND LISTEN MORE.

The church is catching up with Jesus. And we are catching up with the way things are now.

Pressure doesn't work like it used to. Force doesn't work like it used to. Flaring our expertise feathers like birds seeking to impress a potential mate doesn't work like it used to.

Threats don't work like they used to. Assertions of higher knowledge don't work like they used to. So we should stop relying on them like we used to. Especially in matters of religion.

We should make room for our curiosity. We should bristle less and listen more. We should learn to converse and compare notes and share understandings and experiences and interpretations of experiences and theories and evidences.

Truth still matters. For a while, we tried to dispose of truth as a category. But our brains won't let us. We are story-seeking, story-generating, story-telling units, and we cannot help it. And we sort the stories by whether or not they resonate.

We are all on a pilgrimage, even if right now it feels like one to no place in particular. The burden of deciding where to go rests with each of us and with all of us. The only step that matters is the next one. Take it in the hopes that when you do

WE ARE ALL ON A PILGRIMAGE.

you'll be in a better position to see what the next one will be.

Converse with others along the way. Make inquiries of others and respond to their inquiries. Tell the story of your life as you know it. Listen to the stories of others. When you hear a story that burns within you, pay special attention.

For better or worse, we're connected. We're traveling together. We're trying to figure this thing out for ourselves. We're trying to figure it out together. Love is our only hope.

JESUS BRAND SPIRITUALITY STUDY QUESTIONS: COMMUNAL DIMENSION

If you are discussing these questions in a group, you may want to refer to the Discussion Ground Rules for guidance. These can be found in the appendix.

1. How do you think you've been affected by what the author describes as "the myth of individualism" or what Robert Putnam describes as "the loss of social capital"[see pp. 184–87]?

2. What opportunities do you see in your own life to participate more meaningfully in the communal dimension of spirituality?

3. What one thing about the church (your own, those you know of, or your impression of the church at large) would you change to make it more in keeping with the spirituality of Jesus as you understand it?

4. Do you see any difference between saying, "God is loving," and "God is love"?

5. What differences do you see between a spirituality that seeks understanding and one that seeks mastery? Have you ever felt that your approach to spirituality was more about seeking mastery than understanding? Describe what that was like.

AFTERWORD

WHAT IT ALWAYS COMES DOWN TO

When I first encountered Jesus brand spirituality, I became interested enough to start asking questions about what it means to take a step toward the center as one committed to the path.

One of my questions had to do with whether believing that the Jesus path was correct and every other path incorrect was required. "If it's right for me," I asked, "does that mean it's right for everybody?"

Brian, who sat across the table from me, might have answered my question according to the terms of the question itself. He might have said, "Yes, it's right for everybody, which means it's right for you," or "No, it's right for you, but there are many paths that lead to God, and the Jesus path is but one."

Instead, he simply said, "Do you think he's bidding you to follow him?"

"Yes," I replied, aware of the import of my response.

"Well, then, that's what you're being asked to do. Nothing more, nothing less."

Brian gave me the existential answer, and I've come to believe it's the wisest one. It worked for me then and still does to this day.

We can claim all sorts of things, but that doesn't make them so. We can claim to know absolutely that Jesus is the path for everyone. Or we can claim to know (absolutely?) that there are many paths to the same destination. Each claim assumes that the person making the claim stands in an objective position, one outside of existence, where an "objective, unbiased" answer can be given to a question like this.

AT THE MOMENT WE BELIEVE WE ARE BEING SUMMONED TO FOLLOW, NOTHING MATTERS BUT THE PARTICULARS.

If you are convinced that you are able to stand outside of existence in that way in order to make claims of that sort, claim away. I don't for a moment think such a thing is possible.

At the moment we believe we are being summoned to follow, nothing matters but the particulars. Each of us decides whether our own existence is real or illusory. Our deciding it doesn't necessarily make it so, but we have no way to prove it one way or the other. When we choose to believe that we exist, or to act as though we do, life becomes charged with meaning. We are standing within life as participants, not outside of it as observers. And the life we stand within is our particular life, the life we perceive ourselves to be living at this particular time and place, within whatever story we perceive ourselves to be in.

This much I know: I have chosen to believe that I exist, and this choice has made my life meaningful. I believe that I have been summoned to follow Jesus, and I have surrendered and continue to surrender to that summons. I believe that part of being called to follow involves being called to share, to bear witness to this path.

I am called to make the path that I know known to others so that as many as are summoned may also follow.

I don't claim to know this objectively, because I don't believe it's possible for me to stand outside of existence in the way I would need to in order to achieve objectivity.

STANDING WITHIN LIFE, WE CHOOSE. THIS IS WHAT IT MEANS TO BE ALIVE AS A HUMAN BEING.

Standing outside of existence, were it possible, doesn't seem in the least attractive to me because I think the meaning of existence is within it, not outside of it. While I don't claim to know this objectively, I do claim to know this truly. Standing within life, we choose. This is what it means to be alive as a human being.

When I decided to surrender for the first time to the summons I perceived from Jesus, I was pretty nervous about informing Mark, one of my best friends at the time. Mark was smarter than I was and a more adept debater. We enjoyed recreational arguing, and most of the time, if there was a winner, it was Mark. Mark grew up in a different religious tradition than Christianity, but at the time he was a convinced atheist.

Mark was away on a trip to Europe when I took the plunge into Jesus faith. When I picked him up at the airport, I was shocked and relieved to see a New Testament in his carry-on luggage along with a book that I had read in his absence, *Mere Christianity*, by C. S. Lewis.

I figured God was smoothing my path with Mark.

So I spoke openly to Mark about the choices I had made recently to follow. He poked and prodded for quite some time at my new-found faith, peppering me with challenging questions. Finally, he announced to me, "As long as there is even one person in hell, I could never enjoy the pleasures of heaven."

He stumped me there, because it sounded like a sentiment more Christian than Christ. But it assumed, of course, that he was in a position he wasn't in. It assumed that he could know things he couldn't know.

I don't know if I realized this or not. I do know that my immediate response, which was certainly not well thought out or something you'd learn in a course on Christian apologetics, was to call his statement what I perceived it to be: "Bulls----." Oddly, Mark seemed to accept my crude assessment as valid.

We sat together in a long silence. It felt to me as though both of us were being summoned. Eventually, he followed, and he has been on pilgrimage for the decades since.[1]

Looking back, if there was any wisdom in my response, it was the wisdom that says we only have the particulars of our own existence to make choices about, starting with the choice to assume our existence to be real rather than illusory. Everything else is just conjecture, to clean up my language a little.

On the pilgrims' path, the only important step is the next one.

---

1. For Mark Kinzer's current view on the question of eternal destinies, see his paper, "Final Destinies: Qualifications for Receiving an Eschatological Inheritance," http://www.boroughparksymposium.com.

APPENDIX

DISCUSSION GROUND RULES

Spirituality touches on some of the most tender aspects of a person's heart. It's important, therefore, for any group discussion of the material in this book to be guided by some shared understandings in advance. Toward that end, the following ground rules for group discussion could be discussed and agreed upon by the group (and briefly reviewed before each session); even if it seems to be a little awkward to bring it up at first, this kind of shared understanding, made explicit, will often be appreciated by the participants.

1. **What's shared in the group stays in the group.**
   Participants need to know that the thoughts, feelings, and perspectives shared in the group setting won't be shared by others outside of the group, except with specific permission. This applies to everything shared in the group, not simply intimate personal details that might be shared.

2. **No one is expected to share on any given topic; it's fine to pass.**

   While discussion takes a willingness on the part of group participants to speak, no one in the group should feel compelled to speak on any given issue. This freedom allows participants to relax, which leads to better discussions.

3. **No unsolicited advice giving is allowed.**

   Good discussions require great listening. It's often a temptation to jump in with advice when participants share personal struggles. But unsolicited advice giving—even when the advice is good—will often inhibit open sharing. It's the responsibility of group members to ask for advice if they want it. Each time.

4. **Take your fair share of the time.**

   Those who speak up easily and share freely should be encouraged to leave space for those more hesitant to speak, by not hogging the airspace. Think of the group time as a pie; if there are eight members of the group, each slice of the time pie is roughly one-eighth of the time allotted.

5. **Be respectful of the viewpoints of others.**

   It is understood from the outside that each participant has unique experiences and perspectives. The point of the discussion is to share these perspectives freely, respecting different points of view, rather than attempting to arrive at a predetermined consensus or enforce a particular point of view.

ACKNOWLEDGMENTS

I beg the curious reader's indulgence in the inclusion of acknowledgments, which always seem to make of a book more than it truly is.

To my children (and their spouses)—Jesse, Veronica, Maja, Patrick, Amy, Ben, Judy, and Grace—for what they variously accepted, rejected, and altered in my pursuit of spirituality. Some of my best course corrections had them in mind. Now I have the pleasure of learning from their own pursuits and continue to be motivated to live up to them.

To my sisters, Marilyn and Nancy, and my siblings-in-law—Pat, Denise, Kit, Nick, and David—for bearing with my learning curve on the Jesus path in the early years. For Bill Elkington and Rick Rykowsi, for long conversations aimed at figuring things out.

To my parents and in-laws, all now passed away—Glen, Blanche, Stan, and Dolores. I can only underestimate their influence, but I'm grateful for what I realize.

To my fellow pastors and staff at the Vineyard Church of Ann

Arbor—Don Bromley, Donnell Wyche, Mike and Phili Brooks, Marcia Thaxton, Jamie Hartman, Pam Lewis, Jen Buckley, and interns and lay leaders—for keeping the home fires burning while I was writing and helping create a work and church environment I'd enjoy even if I wasn't being paid.

To the people at Thomas Nelson Publishers, for their willingness to risk their good name and business plan on this and every other never-been-before book. Tami Heim, for using the phrase "Jesus brand spirituality" to describe our church to her colleagues at Borders Books and thereby alerting me to its possible value despite its quirkiness. Matt Baugher, Jennifer McNeil, and Jen Stair, for reading, aiding, and abetting the manuscript; Greg Maclachlan and his design team, for their original and, I think, compelling cover; Emily Sweeney, Stephanie Newton, and Kristi Johnson for getting the word out and the all-important Nelson sales team, especially Julie Jayne for saving us all from a lousy subtitle and David McGee for reading and liking the book. And for three women who introduced me to a wider world of publishing—Phyllis Tickle, whose influence is scattered throughout the manuscript; Donna Kehoe, who helped me think soberly about the enterprise of writing a book; and Kathryn Helmers, without whom none of this would have come to pass. (Anyone who thinks little of the profession and calling of literary agency should be ashamed of themselves.)

Also, to the one woman to whom this book is dedicated—Nancy Wilson, my wife.

And to those four, now unnamed people I had especially in mind as readers when I wrote this book. I'll tell you who you are if it sells.

ABOUT THE AUTHOR

Ken Wilson is the Senior Pastor of Vineyard Church of Ann Arbor (www.annarborvineyard.org) and a member of the Vineyard National Board, serving as Regional Overseer of the Great Lakes Region. Ken is active in Scientists and Evangelicals United to Protect Creation, and other efforts to awaken environmental concern in the faith community. Ken and his wife Nancy, have five children.

More information on *Jesus Brand Spirituality* is available on the book's website, at www.jesusbrandspirituality.com. The website includes materials for using the book as an introductory class in spirituality.

You can read Ken's blog at www.kenwilsononline.com.

INDEX

INDEX

INDEX

INDEX

religious right, 23
religious zeal, 17
renewalist quadrant, 25–26, 26nn12–14, 31–32, 34–35, 91
repairing the world, 72–73, 143–144, 163–164
resurrection of Jesus, 51–52, 51n7, 57, 139–140
Rhodenhiser, James, 32
rivers, 135, 136, 138–144
Roman Catholicism, 21, 25, 35n19, 150, 151
Roman occupation forces, 44, 54, 54n13
Rome, 35, 47

Sabbath, observance of, 149
sacred community, 168–171
sacred experience, 168–171
sacred reason, 168–171
sacred Scripture, 168–171
sacred Spirit, 168–171
sacrifice, 155–164, 160n8
Saddleback Community Church, 183–184
Saul of Tarsus, 49, 167
scientific method, 104–106
Scripture, 168–171. *See also* Bible
Serenity Prayer, 118
set prayers, 118–120
sharks, 105–106
Shema, 117
simplicity, 165–166, 171
single moms and families, 49–50
"Slow Train Coming" (Dylan), 63
social capital, 182–186
social justice quadrant, 25, 31–32, 34–35
soul, creation of, 177–181
soul mending, 80–84
South Africa, Truth and Reconciliation Commission, 55–56

Speth, James Gustave, 59–60
spiritual experience
    brain capacity for, 92–93
    contemporary viewpoint of, 90–92
    Pentecostal emphasis on, 22
    worldview lenses and, 93–96
spirituality. *See also* Jesus brand spirituality
    concept of, 9, 10
    generic, 5
    impact of on recovery from addictions, 81–84, 118–119, 120
    use and abuse of, 7
statements of faith, 61–66, 63n2
stillness, 122–125
stories, 133–134, 205–210
string theory, 111
substitutionary atonement, 155–164
suffering, 161–164
suicide prevention work, 68–69
sustainer, 15n12

tears, 139–143
temples
    Ezekiel's garden-temple vision, 137–138
    Herod's, 138–139
Tickle, Phyllis, 7–8, 107–108, 119, 119n7
trademark infringement, 6, 7
transcendent dimension, 100
transubstantiation, 62n1
Trinity, 63n2, 179–180
trust, 135–136, 143, 168
truth, 209
Tutu, Desmond, 55, 91, 190

United Methodists, 25

Vineyard, 30
violence, breaking cycle of, 53–57
vulnerable, care for, 49–50